BIG PIKE

BIG PIKE

Edited by Bob Church

**Contributors: Gord Burton, Neville Fickling,
Mike Green and Barrie Rickards**

The Crowood Press

First published in 2006 by
The Crowood Press Ltd
Ramsbury, Marlborough
Wiltshire SN8 2HR

www.crowood.com

British Library Cataloguing-in-Publication Data
A catalogue record for this book is available from the British
Library.

ISBN 1 86126 858 0
EAN   978 1 86126 858 7

Typeset by Jean Cussons Typesetting, Diss, Norfolk

Printed and bound in Great Britain by Cromwell Press, Trowbridge, Wiltshire

Contents

Eddie Turner with a superb 30lb 8oz pike, one of several over 30lb that he has caught over the years.

Foreword

by Eddie Turner

When Bob Church asked me to write a foreword to this fascinating book on pike fishing, I thought even then that the characters who have contributed to it needed very little introduction, to say the least. What can I say about this merry band of outcasts? Very few sports or pastimes have such a variety and knowledge as the one we enjoy. From a boxer to a doctor, but despite the different backgrounds that we come from, we all have one thing in common … pike fishing. One thing about pike fishing is that there are so many ways to fish for them, each on its own merit being successful. But I've yet to meet the pike man that can perform all the definitions successfully. From bank fishing to boat, from live baiting to fly each has its own experts. The books contributors are among the best in their chosen fields.

To start with, I would like to say just a few words about Bob Church. Our paths have crossed on a few occasions and he is an inspiration, a wealth of knowledge, and last but not least, a well accomplished pike fisherman. I well remember hearing about his exploits on the Fens in my early days when I was a complete novice (still am to some extent, you never stop learning), I take my hat off to you Bob!

Now here's a name – Dr Barrie Rickards; he's probably forgotten more about piking than most people know. Older than Father Christmas himself. By some folk I have become a guru (not a legend yet), but Barrie has gone two steps further – he is an icon. It was because of him that my love of pike fishing grew. The book he wrote together with Ray Webb was the single biggest influence in my pike fishing career. I well remember reading it, and at last fishing for pike began to make sense. His detailed studies and knowledge of the species started a whole new breed of pike fishermen: the dark ages were over, introducing the thinking man pike anglers. Amongst the old school of pike anglers who still regard it as the bible. I don't think it will ever be bettered; improved upon, yes, but not bettered. Caps off to you Barrie, you started the ball rolling.

If pike fishing was ever put into the Wild West days the number 1 in my book would be this character, along with Wild Bill Hickok and Jesse James. Gord Burton has done it. What can be said about Gord that hasn't already been said? A living legend in his own mind at that! As fast as a bullet and crafty as a fox, Gord's been there and done it, got the Tee shirt and the DVD. His input to lure fishing and his adventures on those big wild waters is second to none. Controversial, self-opinionated in his case go hand in hand. It wouldn't be Gord otherwise. Never has a pike angler shown such enthusiasm for the sport. His famous whoops of joy still ring loud and clear: a truly living legend. His exploits on Lomond and the Lake District are myths. Again we have met on several occasions and swapped stories, even as far back as the days when I fished with Bill Hancock, we often met up at conferences; Bill and Gord could talk for England, trying to outdo each other with their stories. His knowledge of those big, big waters and wild piking can only be described as breathtaking. When he gives a slide show or talk you are reliving the experience, such is the enthusiasm of the man. The chapters are truly awe-inspiring, and it makes you want to go pike fishing right here and now.

If Barrie is the godfather, Neville must the godmother. Neville has become Mr Pike over the last few years. I have come to know him fairly well, and have great respect not only for his achievements but also for his enthusiasm. If the X factor for pike fishing could be bottled up, enthusiasm would be the main ingredient. Neville is Mr Statistic (I still manager to tease him on a regular basis about his list). His knowledge and understanding of pike is just phenomenal. I sometimes wonder how he keeps going and going. Sometimes the lure fishing seems to confuse him and often he'll fall asleep shortly after a few casts, but that is mainly an age thing.

He is always the first to the venue, never one to be beaten. In his old age he has become a lot more humorous, and seems to be more relaxed than before. His uncomplicated approach to his fishing and his dogged determination is legendary. Our paths have crossed many times over the years up and down the country, and I even went on holiday with him to Lomond. We will get him up the pub one day, and that's a promise. For the beginner there is a lot to be learned from his writings, and he is a regular contributor to *Pike and Predators* magazine. He is controversial, and is never one to hold back – which does get him into a few spots now and again. He lets his fishing do the talking. The day he relaxes is the day Neville stops going, and the pike world would be a sadder place without him. The author of several books, he has gained a place in pike angling history by catching more 20lb pike than anybody else. It will be etched on his tombstone.

Last but not least is Mike Green, and nearly the youngest of the pack. Mike is one of the most accomplished fly and lure fisherman around. He is quite an unassuming character but boy can he catch fish on those flies. Mike loves the country, has a passion for pike fishing, and has caught some very large pike.

Dedication

We, the authors, dedicate this book to the memory of the late, great pike angler Fred Wagstaffe. He pioneered pike fishing in the big lochs of Scotland, and also the very big loughs of Ireland.

Acknowledgements

First, thanks to my four excellent contributors. They really have given it their best shot, as you will read. Julie Emerson writes her poems in about half an hour; let me give you a quick example: 'Julie, you don't know enough about pike to do me a poem for my new *Big Pike* book, do you?' Half an hour later her husband John rings up to read the pike poem. It's a gift you have, Julie: thanks. Once again I must thank my daughter-in-law Kay Church for typing my chapter. Many thanks to Eddie Turner for writing the interesting Foreword. Eddie knows the capabilities of all the contributors, Eddie himself is, of course, one of the most successful big pike anglers ever. Thanks to EMAP *Angling Times*, and Kevin Clifford of *Coarse Angling Today* magazine, who have published various articles of mine over the years.

Lastly, everyone loves studying a records list, so thanks to Dave Lumb and the Pike Anglers' Club of Great Britain for allowing me to print their list of over 40lb pike.

Esox lucius

Julie Emerson

Esox roams the rivers and lakes,
Her eyes observing others' mistakes,
Patiently waiting and lurking unseen,
Observing perch, roach and bream.
Planning her attack with such accurate speed,
Her instincts are … just simply to feed.

One swift premeditated attack will surely provide
The meal that she needs and fulfil her will to survive.
Preying on fish that have no way to defend,
One snap of her jaw … and that is the end.
Silently stalking and searching out prey
that will ensure her survival for another day.

Lucius is purely a feeding machine.
A predator of ancient esteem …
Her ancestry dates her way back in the past …
Before anglers had made their first ever cast.
She's as old as the rivers in which she patrols …
She seeks out her targets and hunts for the shoals.

Esox is capable of achieving great age.
She installs fear into her prey and attacks them with rage.
But she is graceful and sleek as she instinctively feeds
As her will to survive surpasses her needs
Longevity ensure that her size is immense.
Her only weakness is the anglers' intent.

When the tables are turned and the hunter becomes prey …
Many pike anglers will dream of that day.
The day that a double takes hold of their bait,
The day that their scales can witness her weight
Photographs taken to cherish with pride …
And back to the depths *Esox* will glide.

About the Authors

by Bob Church

I was very careful in my choice of the four anglers for this third-in-line series book, this time on big pike. All are very well known in the world of pike fishers, and I have rubbed shoulders with them over the years, and know well of their skills and capabilities.

Dr Barrie Rickards from Cambridge is a father figure in pike-fishing circles, and has a great many big pike catches behind him. It was Barrie who found out that if you try and get rid of pike from a trout water by removing or killing the few big ones, all you get is about ten times as many pike of around 3lb to 8lb. Now, this is a far worse problem for the trout fisher than a few big old pike. So please, any would-be culler of pike, leave them and allow nature to look after things in her own way, because big pike eat enormous numbers of small jack pike. So I would argue that a few big pike are actually good for a trout fishery – or any fishery, for that matter. Barrie covers the history of pike fishing in his chapter.

My current piking companion is Mike Green, a retired optician from Northampton. Mike and I have taken some incredible pike catches during these past three years. The interesting thing is, that 95 per cent of our best catches have all fallen to artificials. We shared some magnificent sport on Jerkbait outfits, also on big copper and silver spoons. Nevertheless, our best efforts in high number catches usually come on our fly tackle. I have designed a special 9ft Champions pike fly rod, which is stiff and casts a No. 12 shooting head some fifty yards. You need this power and weight of fly line to cast the flies; the ones that we use are up to 9in in length. You will learn all there is to know about artificials from Mike.

Neville Fickling is from the Fens, and is an extremely determined hunter of big pike, travelling all over the country and Ireland in search of the big ones. Recently he fished both Sweden and Spain to catch some fine pike to add to his never-ending list of twenty-pounders. Neville covers live- and deadbait methods, and tells of his successes with big pike while using these tactics. He might even name some of his favourite waters for you to try (I think he is mellowing as he gets older).

Finally there is Gord Burton from Southport: what a character this fellow is! His enthusiasm for pike fishing in general is definitely catching. Recently he gave a talk/slide show to the Northampton Specimen Group, which was an enormous success. His pike-fishing adventures are all in this chapter, and some of his encounters with Lake Windermere and Loch Lomond pike are very exciting indeed. In fact, Gord will be relating a great many of his red-letter days; but importantly, he will explain exactly how he did it, so you can try it, too.

1. Pike, a Life-long Fascination

by Bob Church

I remember to this day seeing my first pike as a young boy of about eight years old. It was lying in the rushes of a gin-clear pool that was connected to the upper River Nene near to Chapel Brampton. Although it must only have been about 4lb in weight, at the time it looked to me such a fearsome beast! From then on I always had an interest in pike fishing during the then traditional season of 1 October until 14 March. In my teens I moved up in size: first with a 10lb fish – what a breakthrough that was! – and then another of 13½lb, all from Horton little village lake.

In 1963 I met up with the late Fred Wagstaffe, who was fast making a name for himself. He had caught a 28½lb pike from Sywell reservoir, spinning with a 9in wobbled silver spoon. In Northampton at the time there were about ten friends, all of whom loved fishing for specimen fish, so we formed the Northampton Specimen Group. As I write, and some forty-two years later, it is still possibly the top group in the country. In 1966–7 Fred was making regular trips to the Norfolk Broads mostly at Heigham Sounds, Hickling Broad and Horsey Mere. He caught plenty of big pike over 25lb and up to just over 30lb.

I remember in October 1967 that four of us from the group decided to go to Horsey Mere for a weekend trip after pike: Phil Shatford, Rod Kilsby, Ray Clay and myself. We hired two motor boats from Martham yard, and in pouring rain

motored off along Cardle Dyke in search of Horsey Mere. The rain was torrential and we tackled up as we motored along; I was in the boat with Phil, and Ray shared with Rod. Because Fred had told us what to expect we had a good idea what to do, but he did say, 'It's fishing OK, but the bigger ones have not been feeding.'

Our two boats motored into Horsey and we crept quietly into the first big bay on the left side. We all cast out our baits, fished suspended under a float set at about three feet deep, so the bait worked just above the thick submerged weedbeds. I remember it well: it was still pouring with rain, but Ray's bait was taken immediately he cast out, and he was playing a 26½-pounder. At the same time I had struck into a 22½-pounder. What a great start as this was: my first 20lb-plus pike! Later Rod had a nineteen-pounder and Phil a 19½-pounder, as well as plenty of back-up fish; and then the feeding spell ended. I was soaked to the skin, but very happy – in the first few minutes of being introduced to the Mere we had enjoyed the cream: certainly a lasting memory.

I used to try all manner of lures, spoons or spinners, and some rather pathetic plugs when judged by today's standards. I caught very little on them, except perhaps on the No. 5 Mepps in both gold and silver blades. I was catching a great many pike on fly from the big trout reservoirs, but because I was really after trout, I didn't value

Bob's first 20lb-plus pike, at 22½lb. It came from Horsey Mere on the Norfolk Broads. It poured with rain all day.

them very highly. Even so, I did get my first twenty-pounder on the fly – or in fact 6in white tandem lure, meant for big trout; it weighed 21lb 12oz, and came from Grafham Water in the early seventies. To be honest I felt at the time that livebait was the way for the best pike sport. No matter which water I fished, livebait produced not only the most fish, but also the heaviest specimens; this was my main approach, and that of my piking friends of the time.

In about 1971, a small group of us from the Northampton Specimen Group began to fish in Fenland. Jim Shrive, Mike Prorok, Geoff Smith, Gordon Labrum and myself would go every weekend from October to March, and we had some very good sport. The waters we concentrated on were the 'Sixteen-foot Drain' and the River Delph, which we found were by far the best; we also occasionally fished the Old Bedford river or the Middle Level.

The 1972 to 1973 pike season was one of the best I can remember, and nearly every weekend we 'hit the jackpot'. Jim Shrive and I found the Sixteen-foot Drain

The 1970s and Bob had this twenty-one-pounder on fly at Grafham.

BELOW: The perfect pike-fishing day. This is Dick Shrive whom I fished with on the middle-level drain. Between us we caught eighteen pike to 14lb.

by mistake: we had fished the Twenty-foot Drain unsuccessfully in the morning, but had caught quite a few baits; so we drove off, went through Chatteris, and turned on to the road where the Sixteen-foot ran alongside it for miles.

We drove along for a while and kept looking until we found a perfect spot to get the car well off the narrow road; later we named it the 'Jenny Gray' farm swim. That afternoon – pre-Christmas 1971 – was the start of some terrific Fenland pike sessions: in three hours' fishing with roach live- and deadbaits, on free rover and drift light float tackle, we caught ten pike. It was a very lively session, and I was more than pleased with a 24½lb pike; Jim's best went 13lb.

Jim and I returned to the same swim on the Sixteen-foot Drain a week later; it was Boxing Day 1971. Jim started the ball rolling with a very lively seventeen-pounder, which bent the arm of our large landing net and caused it to collapse. Then in mid-afternoon I hooked a 17½-pounder,

followed by my best-ever pike of 31½lb, which took my skimmer bream livebait and made off on a long run up the centre of the drain. Scores of roach leapt out of the water in fright. I was determined to play this fish out carefully, because we had a high bank and a broken landing net to contend with. This I did, and when the pike surfaced and lay in the shallows beaten, it looked every bit like a young crocodile in some jungle swamp.

For its recovery I have to thank Jim, who jumped into the icy, thankfully fairly shallow water in his shoes and up to his knees. Holding the landing net arms wide, somehow between us we managed to guide it into the net, and scrambled up to the higher flat bank and laid the fish on the long wet grass. We then discovered that it was only hooked by one hook of a small treble in the corner of the mouth, and this was almost straightened; I was able to return the fish completely unmarked. It was an angling memory I shall never

Bob shows his best-ever pike at 31½lb. It fell to livebait from the Sixteen-foot Drain near Jenny Gray's farm, on 26 December 1972.

Trout waters are very productive as pike grow on quickly in them. This is at Ringstead Grange. Edward Foster is on the left with a 27lb fish, and Bob's was 20½lb.

forget. Remember, 30lb pike get caught quite often from various stocked trout waters, but thirty-pounders from non-trout waters are really in a different class.

As an aside, for this reason alone it is my feeling that where record pike weights are to be shown, they should regularly publish two lists, one for trout-stocked waters and the other for non-trout-stocked waters. This is because we all now know that pike that live in the trout lakes pack on an incredible weight very quickly on a regular rainbow diet. Do you agree?

To return to Fenland, my friends and I had many more great catches of pike, and also zander, in the next few years. It was when fishing on the incredible River Delph that I had some big catches of good-sized pike – and saw others have good catches, too. I say 'incredible' River Delph because every so often during summer this water suffers from a natural kind of pollution. After heavy rainstorms, the adjacent rich grassland washes all fill up quickly, and in warm summer weather the water-covered grass soon begins to ferment and cause the water to de-oxygenate; then it runs back into the Delph and kills most of the fish, including the pike. This had happened in 1968 – yet only seven years later it produced some of the best (non-trout) piking I have ever seen. I'll quote you just a few examples of what took place.

We found the stretch at the lower end of the River Delph; known as the Post Office Mile, it began to produce good catches regularly, for all of us. We used to approach this section by driving down a farmer's drove and then pulling ourselves across the narrow Old Bedford river on a flat punt; that morning, however, someone had left all the two-way pulley system on the far bank, so it appeared we could not get across. Undaunted, I set up my pike rod with a 2oz bomb and a couple of trebles snap tackle, and cast this across and straight into the boat. It hooked up first cast, and I then gently winched the boat across. Once on the right bank, I got down to the serious business of catching fish, along with my colleagues Mike Prorok and Gordon Labrum.

We had some small roach livebaits, and these soon produced a couple of pike for me of 7lb and 5lb. Then my line broke on the strike, and on investigating I found my rod had developed a badly damaged ring that now had a sharp edge. I quickly cut through the whipping with my penknife and removed it, re-tackled up, and moved on to a new swim where the angler was just packing up. He had blanked on sea dead-baits, so I decided to use the largest livebait I had: a 4oz roach.

Within seconds of the float settling I had a fast run and was playing a big fish. Then I realized I had left my landing net in the previous swim, some 200 yards away; but Mike Prorok was close by to help out, and when I brought the fish in for the last time, well beaten, he was able to chin it, landing it gently by hand: a glorious river pike of 25lb 12oz. For the rest of that day we had other fish to low doubles.

They say that lightning never strikes twice in the same place; however, I don't believe that any more. Mike Gordon and I returned to the same place on the Delph

A superb 25¾lb pike from the River Delph in Fenland.

Mike Prorok returns his 25½lb pike to the River Delph.

Sometimes a big zander like this 10¼lb specimen takes the bait intended for pike. This is often the case in Fenland, where this was caught by Bob at Roswell Pit, Ely.

the following weekend, but this time settled in about a mile away; as we drove along Mike said, 'It's my turn this week!' And within an hour of fishing this new spot Mike had a run, and I landed a 25½lb pike for him; it had fought very hard. At that moment the Anglian water bailiff arrived, John McAngus, and admired the fish. About an hour later came a second run for Mike, and he hooked into what he thought was a good double-figure pike – but what a surprise we were in for.

As the fish fought strongly Mike caught a glimpse of it just beneath the surface, and yelled 'It's a zander!'. After playing it really carefully it was netted by the bailiff John, who was on his return walk. At that time this zander was a very rare specimen fish. It had taken a 4oz roach livebait, and weighed in at 11½lb, which easily set a new species record for the water; also Mike raised the Northampton Specimen Group record by more than 4lb. While all this was going on I was having superb sport, with ten pike caught to 13½lb – so I was not

complaining, and Gordon had two more, as well: between us we totalled well over 100lb of pike. After this period zander began to spread all over the Fens, and we had good sport with them, too, in the years that followed.

Without doubt the best catch from the River Delph that I knew about that season fell to those lively characters from the Coventry Circus group. Similar to us, they fished livebaits on free river float, and then worked their way downriver, overlapping two rods each as they moved; this is a great method for searching out pockets of pike. I had other pike of 23lb and 21½lb while fishing in this way, and I also witnessed Dennis Moules catch a beautiful pike of 28½lb near Welney Bridge. It still works today if you are young enough to do it, though remember you have to carry the livebait bucket and other kit, too, as you go. The Coventry lads had their catch where the river bends at the end of the Post Office Mile. The best fish went to Dave Malin at 33½lb; then Derek Brown's best

Dennis Moules from Cambridge with another tremendous specimen pike from the prolific River Delph; weight 28½lb.

Bob plays a lively fish on the Delph; here it was almost in flood.

Ray Brown lands Dave Malin's great pike of 33½lb from the downstream end of the Post Office Mile, on the River Delph.

fish went to 26lb 6oz, his brother Ray Brown followed with a best of 25lb 2oz, and finally Lol Derricot's best went 14¾lb, along with several other good fish that day; it was the best catch the River Delph had ever had. And by the way, the three big ones were all being played at the same time.

In the years that have followed I have pike fished all over the place. Lough Allen in Ireland was very good; I would highly recommend it. I had two or three trips there, with great results for my fishing friends – and I didn't do too badly myself, either. Alan Pearson took a near-30lb fish on a trolled plug, while Frank Cutler had a 22lb pike, Paul Harris a 22½-pounder and Jeanette, my wife, and I had fifteen-pounders. All fell to trolling, except Paul and I fished the famous spawning bay known as Frizzels where we had several doubles and one twenty-pounder.

Livebaiting and, just occasionally, static deadbait fishing was my main approach to

catching big pike about five years ago. That was when my good friend Mike Green and I started to fish in earnest for pike with artificials, mainly fly fishing, which we pioneered, and jerkbait fishing, which still fascinates me. That final lunge from the pike is so spectacular – and I have even had them grab the jerk as it leaves the water.

These days I do fully appreciate catching pike on the fly and jerk, or even on a big spoon. Everything is more straightforward, as we have a much greater choice of gravel-pit fisheries to fish; for example, in my area they are scattered throughout the whole Nene and Great Ouse valleys, from source to sea. These are mostly the waters I concentrate on, together with a few big reservoir boat trips – and even the rivers when they are fishing nice and clear in the winter months.

Really, it has only been in the last five years that I have concentrated all my effort into lure and fly fishing – though it does help to have a wildly enthusiastic fishing partner who has retired, like myself. I refer to Mike Green, who makes some of the most marvellous fly lure patterns. Between us, we have caught a lot of pike – and big pike too.

Sometimes it's fly tackle that catches the most fish, and we always begin the session by using these lovely flies tied on 0/6 single big hooks, with a fairly long shank (illustrated in the photos in Mike Green's selection). Even so, I always have the jerk and copper spoon tackle made up ready, and with this approach I caught six fish that were over 20lb in weight last year (2003). The account below describes a few examples of what can be achieved – red letter days, really.

First there was a day's boat fly fishing for pike with trout angler John Emerson. We were out on Grafham water, fishing the Hill Farm bay beyond the North Aeriation tower. During the morning I dropped three fish, probably double-figure pike or zander, when they 'let go' of the fly; I learnt that day always to strike a second and even

a third time to make sure the big 6/0 fly hook had a firm hold. Sometimes when you are losing fish, it is because the pike are merely gripping the fly with their jaws, and when they realize that all is not well, they open their mouth and the fly falls out – so remember, always give that extra big strike.

By the time it came to lunchtime I had caught a pike of 8lb, a good perch of 2¾lb, and even a 6.5lb bream. John had taken several big perch. Also fishing for pike close by was Andy Goram, a really keen pike-on-fly angler from Suffolk; he was catching quite well.

John and I moved the boat to a new anchoring position, and sat quietly eating our sandwiches and having a cup of tea. We both had fast-sinking lines on, John was using a tandem No. 6 Appetiser lure, and I had changed up to an all-silver sparkly tube fly tied on top of a baby's nose bud tube. These are very thick and strong, and so I risked not having a wire trace; besides, the tube had only a small hole in it and my

Again at Grafham: when using big flies for pike you catch wonderful specimen perch. This was a 3¼-pounder.

wire traces had a swivel at one end and a link swivel at the other. Obviously these would not go through the hole, so I left it, thinking the pike would not bite through the thick plastic; but this was to prove the biggest mistake I ever made in my angling life.

We both made our first cast together, leaving the flies for thirty seconds to reach the bottom before starting the retrieve. But at that moment we both hooked into very heavy fish, which just had to be pike. After about ten minutes' steady pressure, we brought both fish to the surface where we could see they were each around 30lb. To hook one 30lb pike is the achievement of a lifetime; to hook two at the same time is the stuff of dreams!

Panic set in, as we had only one specimen net between us. But we were spared having to decide which fish to net first when mine dived deep and escaped by biting through the plastic tube and nylon. A lesson learned!

I then set about netting John's pike in the 42in-diameter net. The fish was of almost crocodile proportions and had the Appetiser lure firmly in the scissors of its jaws. To safely unhook, weigh and photograph a fish of this size we used a cushioned unhooking mat and hammock weighing sling. The fish went to 30lb 8oz, and swam happily away after its photograph was taken. Big pike need handling with care if you want them to swim away after capture.

Another hour's fishing produced nothing, so we moved spots again. The new mark near Hedge End produced a 6lb 8oz bream on a tandem Appetiser, and gave a long and dogged fight. Big bream feed on fry in autumn, so I was not surprised to catch one. But I still hadn't caught a zander.

Large boobies had been working at Grafham for zander, so I put one on. The zander seemed to respond to a more erratic retrieve, so I really got this fly kicking and jerking a few feet from the bottom. I lost the first two zander I hooked, so I tried giving the fish a couple of extra firm strikes to set the hooks more securely. This worked straightaway, and my first Grafham zander of 4 to 5lb came to the net.

To prove this remarkable day was not a fluke, I followed it up with a second trip the following weekend. This time there were more boats anchored and back-drifting around the tower area – so the word had got out!

Even though the weather was hot and calm on this second trip, I still took a 19lb pike, while John landed a perch of 2lb 10oz and two 6lb bream. Other anglers had several zander, and pike to 18½lb. But what amazed me even more was the fact that not a single trout was caught – and do you know, no one minded! But I will always have in my mind the sheer luck of hooking two thirties together, 'on fly' – and the fact that I definitely blew it!

Having had a day's boat fishing for pike with fly rod first, followed by jerkbait fishing for them, I was most impressed by the effectiveness of the jerk method. Although I reserve the right to do a bit of livebait fishing occasionally, the bulk of my pike fishing nowadays is either fly fishing or the deadly jerkbait fishing. Because both of these methods are so exciting to use, let's investigate them further.

For a start, it is so different from sitting behind two deadbaits fished at long range; you need to cover a good expanse of water continuously with both the fly and jerk methods. This can be from a boat, or just by fishing your way around the lake, covering all the likely spots. If your tackle set-up is correct and you are covering lots of new fish with each cast, you are on your way to a good day's sport. So first, let us look at the tackle requirements.

PIKE ON FLY GEAR

You can get by using the heaviest reservoir trout fly rods available, with weight forward eight or nine lines. I must stress, however, that to do it properly you need to cast specially designed 9in 'fly lures' on size 6/0 single hooks up to forty and even fifty yards. Now that may sound out of your league, but please believe me, it isn't. Because of my experience with various fly rods over forty or so years, I felt qualified to design a pike fly rod for the 2003 season. It's 9ft in length, and takes a no. 11 or 12 shooting head; this is attached to 100m of flat 'Black Streak' special, pre-stretched nylon, and the whole lot is used on a wide-arbor fly reel. This is also a 'must' if you are to avoid tangles.

Because of the stiff power of the rod you need a heavier line to flex it to unleash its power and then carry the large, heavy, feathered lure these great distances. There is a casting style called 'double hauling' that builds up the speed. With the shooting head outside the top rod ring, and another 30m of backing ready to be fired lying evenly on the boat deck or bank, the lure is released, projecting the fly lure as far as you would when spinning with the fixed spool reel. The rod is called the Bob Church Champion pike fly rod.

Mike Green is my regular fishing companion, and during this type of fishing he had some marvellous results using both methods; and so did I, for that matter, every time I went fishing with him. Where fly fishing is concerned we both use five different fly lines for different situations: a floater, naturally, in shallow water; a sink-tip and a slow sinker for depths of up to 12 ft; a medium sinker D1.3; or a very fast sinker D1.7 for deeper water. For example, the D1.7 would be my choice for the 25ft deep hotspots at Grafham water.

Bob shows his best of the day: 19lb 2oz while fly fishing for pike at Chew Valley Lake near Bristol.

As with trout fishing, changing the colour of the lures can turn follow-ups into positive takes. A 19lb 2oz fish from Chew Valley lake in Bristol earlier in the summer put up an incredible tail-walking and gill-flaring fight – but this is what you will all experience if you give this method a try! Remember that your local river, if it is running reasonably clear, will be an ideal place to try fly-piking and to get some good practice in. Most rivers have plenty of 4lb to 7lb pike, and these will give you some good sport if you keep on the move.

During the winter months Mike and I regularly caught fifteen pike in a day. It is all-action fishing because of the continuous casting and retrieving. This style of piking is still in its infancy nationwide, but it is growing fast among enthusiasts. We recently caught ninety pike in a four-hour session from the Nene. I had fifty-six of them on fly and jerk, but Mike took all his thirty-four on fly. We are told by *Angling Times* that this was a record.

JERKBAITING FOR PIKE

Derek McDonald popularized this method a few years back, but for some reason it never caught on with the average fisherman. This included myself, but after hearing about Mike Green's incredible results during a continuous all-winter period, I tried it properly for myself.

The tackle is quite simple: a stiff, one-piece, 6ft rod, combined with a small multiplier reel that doesn't give overrun problems, forms the basis of the tackle required. I use a Shimano Curado (as does Mike) loaded with braid line of 40lb breaking strain, a few rigid special wire traces, and an assortment of jerkbaits.

Jerking seems to be a method which is at its best on waters that are reasonably shallow – up to about 15ft. Gravel pits are perfect because they will have been heavily weeded all summer, and usually have good clarity. I found last year that the decaying weed on the bottom was perfect for pike to lie up in, just watching and waiting for an ambush, and that a jerkbait cast and worked over the top of them was the most effective: the well worked jerk's irregular darting movements seem to prove irresistible to the majority of pike. The only time I found it didn't work was when the water temperatures were at their lowest, for instance following very

hard, frosty periods when the margins and close environs were frozen and hard – only then did I fall back to live- or deadbaits. If you try both or just one of these methods over the winter months, I guarantee you will have some action-packed piking.

Going back about four years ago, Mike and I went fly fishing for pike on a normal non-trout coarse gravel pit in Bucks. Mike said he would also bring along his jerkbait outfit to show me what it was all about, because he had been doing so well with it. For example, he'd had a catch of four pike at 31lb 12oz, 31lb, 28lb 10oz and 18lb from the bank at Blithfield. But let's forget about oversized trout-fed pike for a while: so how would jerkbait perform on the non-trout gravel pits?

Mike had been concentrating on the shallow, clear-water gravel pits of the Great Ouse and Nene river valleys. In the main his approach is to use home-made jerkbaits, which he makes with precision. The commercial ones are quite acceptable, as I discovered for myself, but his do seem to work that much better. We had two gravel-pit sessions fishing together for pike during the Christmas holiday break, and chose a 30-acre pit that remained gin clear, despite the very heavy rains; furthermore, both the air and water temperatures were incredibly high: so when did you last fish on Christmas Eve with air temperatures of 55°F? These were perfect conditions for pike to be on the lookout for food.

Now, in over fifty years of pike fishing, I had never found an artificial bait that could catch pike even half as well as natural baits, lives or deads. And so it was to be, myself using livebait and Mike using his deadly jerks. It was the shortest day of the year, but we managed about six hours' fishing. Using his jerkbaits Mike had nine fish, including some lovely specimens of 13lb 12oz, 15lb 4oz, 18lb 4oz and 23lb

12oz, plus six others between 5lb and 8lb. The roach livebait and deadbait tactics produced a measly three seven-pounders.

It continued to be mild, so both Mike and I were back on New Year's Eve, fishing for most of the day in our jumpers, which was something of a first for me. We both fly fished in the morning and did very well, Mike taking eight fish on fly to a good size of 12lb. Any double-figure pike caught on this tackle gives good sport, and the fight and skills required to land it proved what a good angler Mike is. I had landed four good pike on my fly tackle, all about 5lb to 8lb, but my greatest disappointment came when a fish of well over 20lb followed the fly right to my feet before turning away.

With about an hour and a half of light left I just had to have a serious go at jerkbait fishing. I had kitted myself up with what appears to be the best reel for the job: the Shimano Curado Multiplier. It is foolproof, and even complete beginners cannot get overruns (this was always something that put me off this type of reel with earlier models). To say I was pleased with my next three pike would be an understatement. I had tried a shop-bought jerk for half an hour with only a follow for my efforts, so I asked Mike if I could try one of his silver home-made jerks. I put it on, and had complete confidence that it would catch. First I had a sixteen-pounder, but then had to wait until the light began to fade, when I had two fish in quick succession – a 15¾-pounder, followed by a superb fish of 20½lb that had engulfed the whole jerkbait. Despite this it was only hooked in the mouth tissue, hence it put up an incredible fight.

It seemed that I spent much of the two days taking photographs of Mike, but now it was my turn to do a bit of posing. There is a certain amount of self-congratulation to be done when you catch a twenty-pounder from a non-trout water.

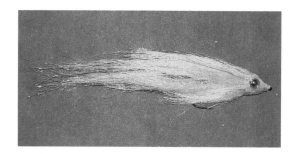

My yellow Canary pike fly 'Deadly': it works at every water we fish at.

If you intend to use three methods in the same day, always begin with fly fishing, as the constant 'heavy metal' casting that can be jerking or big spoons tends to kill off fly fishing. Earlier I explained about the special Champion pike fly rod and fly lines, and the following few items should go with them. I use about 6 to 9ft of 20lb bs nylon for my leader, and to this I attach a nylon-covered trace: this is a stainless-steel wire clip so that I can change fly lure patterns quickly and easily.

The reel has to be a good, big, wide-arbor model. Long before I invented the first wide-arbor reel, the Lineshooter, over thirty years ago, made for me by Mick Willis, I used a wide-drum Ariel coarse trotting reel to do a similar job. The Lineshooter idea has been copied by all fly-reel firms in the years that have followed.

The wide-arbor reels keep any fly line or shooting head from coiling and forming spring-like memory. Narrow-spindled, traditional fly reels are just the opposite, causing bad line-coiling and many tangles, when simply casting. I have tried many backing lines for my long-distance casting when using a shooting head, so can guarantee the following method: I use a pre-stretched, black flat nylon of 30lb bs known as Black Streak; it comes on 100m spools, which is just right. I run out 30m or so on the grass, and ask whoever I am fishing with to hold the end, then we give it a good stretch for a few minutes. If you do this at the start of each day's fishing, there will be no tangle problems.

If you are bank fishing, all you need is a pair of unhooking pliers. Also, the trout fly fisher's idea of a line tray can aid long-distance casting. Perhaps you can get out boat fishing, and I do highly recommend this, especially on the bigger gravel pits and reservoirs; it's a great way to search out the depths, drifting slowly across the lake. I say 'slowly', because in this case another of my trout kit interventions might be useful: the Maxi Boat Drogue. This is put out from the central stern position, and allows the boat to drift, bow first, downwind. After each drift, keep moving the boat over 30m or so, then you will gradually cover the whole lake.

Other equipment for going afloat should be a good life jacket (worn at all times); a good combination unhooking mat/extra-large weigh sling (the Shimano model is great); a landing net of very large diameter; a set of reliable clock-dial weighing scales; and waterproof plasters are for when you inevitably come into contact with the

pike's razor-sharp gill rakers. Don't forget the wide-angle camera, and a complete waterproof outfit: we don't come in, even if it rains for a few hours. I use a comfortable, cushioned boat seat that opens up and sits on top of the gunwales. We also have an electric Minn Kota engine and a portable Fishing Buddy depth sounder and fish finder.

The selection of fly lures has narrowed down somewhat over the last few years; I now use about ten or so patterns (see photographs). Mike Green has made many of these, but anyone can learn to make them quite easily (see Mike's chapter).

A VERY COLD WINTER PIKE SESSION

It was a bitterly cold winter's day. Now, I have to admit that my creaky joints don't really like this sort of day, but Mike's enthusiasm tends to be infectious. Nevertheless, our usually deadly Canary pike fly, the incredible deadly big spoons, and the never-fail special jerks just didn't work in the bitter cold.

This clearly shows how pike take a big fly, in this case Bob's favourite 'Yellow Canary'.

A 'one fish day' Mike predicted. I tempted it with a very small livebait on light tackle (No. 10) hooks. It was a one fish day, but I am glad I caught it: 26lb 6oz!

Mike tried to cheer me up by saying 'It could just be a one-run, big-pike day, so if you get a chance, make the most of it!'. We both changed to the roach livebaits, and I set my float at seven feet, fishing over nine feet of water. As the bait was only small – about six inches – I used a delicate size 10, barbless, two treble rig. This was cast to the side and allowed to drift round with the light wave action. Every few minutes I re-trieved the livebait with a couple of turns of the reel; this raised it up in the water and then dropped it back down again, just like an injured, ailing fish.

When the one and only take of the day came, my float disappeared with a 'plop'. I tightened down, felt that the fish was there, and gave a firm but not manic strike. It was on. After a few seconds it wallowed on the top, and I knew it was 20lb plus; I carefully played it out and Mike netted it aboard at the first attempt. We placed it into the extra-large unhooking mat/weigh sling, and quickly rowed to the bank to weigh and photograph it. At 26lb 6oz it was a new fish from a pit with which we had become fairly familiar. In all fairness, this was the climax to a quite brilliant month of pike fishing.

At risk of becoming boring about fly fishing for pike, here nonetheless is further evidence why pike anglers should try it. In September, when fishing deep for pike at Grafham, I dragged a yellow pike lure from the bottom, in 25ft of water; evidently another angler had been snagged, and had lost it. I tried it, even though it was poorly tied, and I caught some decent pike and perch. I later tried it out at a big pit and caught four more pike and perch before the lure disintegrated, following one too many encounters. Mike was aware of all this and tied a couple up, one for each of us; they were quite easy to make, as the dressing was relatively straightforward. We never looked back.

My first run out was with Hugh Miles and Martin Bowler, filming a new series for BBC Television. I caught nine pike, all on that same yellow Canary pike lure; this included two doubles of 16lb and 11½lb. Mike's best catch on the lure was twelve pike, including five doubles; we also recently shared a catch of sixteen pike for 150lb on another pit – a memorable session. It was very mild on this trip; in fact, it was the third Christmas Eve running when the weather and fishing conditions were perfect for using artificials. This year, however, Mike stayed with the yellow Canary all day, whereas I used spinner tactics – this was mainly because I had found a brand new, but old-fashioned, 3in Colorado spoon amongst my tackle, and wanted to use it, just to see how it would fare against modern lures. Suffice to say I was casting the Colorado a good seventy yards and did very well indeed. I had earlier put in a couple of hours on the big jerks and copper spoons, which usually serve me well, and would normally produce plenty of fish in these conditions – but not on this day. The switch to the smaller Colorado gave me seven decent pike, and best two weighing 13lb and 12lb.

There is a bit of a story attached to these two pike. I caught them both on the Colorado at around midday, and Mike caught the same two on his yellow Canary fly in the afternoon, about two hours later. Both pike had unmistakable identification marks on them. So can we conclude from this that when pike are in feeding mood, nothing will stop them from getting their meal; and if this is the case, maybe it only happens infrequently, perhaps once a week?

Bob shows the size and ferocious mouth of a big pike; when they are on the feed nothing will stop them.

Mike prepares our boat Sneaky *for a day afloat fishing for pike: fly and jerk or spoon, at one of the many gravel pits.*

When the pike are not feeding, it is quite possible to imagine that the pit has no pike in it at all. So when they are 'on the feed' they are fairly easy, but when they are 'off' they are impossible. As I mentioned, December turned out to be excellent for pike. Mike Green kept with the fly all month and had a total of seventy-three pike, the best 20½lb from a pit, and 19lb 6oz from the River Nene. Importantly, we found that the river has to be a certain height and clear before you attempt to fly fish for pike.

As far as my own results go, I caught thirty-three December pike on the Canary fly, the best 16½lb, with twenty others on the jerk and spoons. Just one fish came to a roach bait, but interestingly, and perhaps significantly, it weighed 26lb 12oz.

Mike Green and I have been fishing here and there on a dozen or more gravel pits these last few winters. I found two such pits adjacent to each other that looked worth a try. Nothing happened much for several sessions after pike, until one

November day when Mike caught a 27½-pounder on the deadly jerk bait.

He could not wait to tell me all about it, and his experience fired my enthusiasm to start winter pike fishing for myself, mixing it with the barbel sessions. A couple of days later we set off to the other nearby pit, where we could use a boat (Mike has one and a trailer). We went armed with everything: fly kit, jerk kit, and we would even try bait fishing, if we had to.

We soon found that there were no fish in the shallows on this bright and sunny winter's day, so we caught a dozen small roach livebaits, put all our kit in the boat and rowed out to the deepest areas. We each decided to put out a livebait rod, while Mike fly fished and I jerk fished with the boat at anchor. I soon had some action. A nice fish of 12lb took my livebait at twelve noon, and the same thing happened about ten minutes later, but this time it was a better fish, at 14lb. I was quite pleased. But as Mike took a quick picture of my fourteen-pounder, he said 'Quick Bob, grab the

Mike Green shows his 25lb 8oz pike caught on livebait.

camera, my float's just gone!' He was into a bigger fish – and at 25½lb, what a fish! He was glowing. We rowed into the bank to take some pictures, but this proved to be a mistake, because the big pike of this pit had come to feed together, and we wasted half an hour of their feeding time.

Going out again, Mike cast out his livebait rod first, and the float went straightaway. The result was a 29lb fish! Then it was unhooking, weighing and photographing again. I was becoming a professional ghillie: I had not cast out since catching the fourteen-pounder! However, the time was now 2pm and the pikes' feeding ceased – just like switching off a light. So we had found out that a water that had previously

given us blank sessions held some great pike. Mike finished the day with a 15½-pounder to fly, as we made one final drift across the whole pit.

What a start to the season Mike was having. We hastily arranged another day at another pit for two days later. From our experiences, it was no good hammering a pike water over and over again. Fish it once or twice a month and sport remained good, but if certain waters are fished too often, they soon become ruined, even if top pike men are doing the fishing. More than any other species, pike thrive on neglect. Could Mike do the hat-trick and take another big one? It was certainly a great fishing day, very mild at 54°F, and overcast with a light breeze. Once again we each used bait on one rod, while he fly fished and I jerked with the other. This is a great combination attack for any gravel pit fishery, because sooner or later, one method will succeed.

I set the ball rolling with a 12-pounder to the bait rod, then a follow from a decent fish to my bright orange Helltail jerk lure. I then had another small pike of about 3lb to the bait. We moved for the third time, and Mike started to cast with the fly rod, using one of our new fly creations. We now have some marvellous designs that are light years ahead of anything that has gone before.

As Mike's fly neared the boat, I saw a large pike's head engulf it completely. It then lay motionless for three seconds before its head swelled into a gill-flaring rage and it sped off. The fight began. Watching Mike play yet another good pike confirmed my satisfaction with my new complete fly outfit – I netted his fish at a weight of 21lb 6oz. So the lesson is this: don't go pike fishing without the fly tackle. I can promise you that it is not just a whim, but a very effective pike-catching method –

as long as you have the right rod and flies.

In deepest, coldest winter I had another boat session when everything failed to tempt a take – that is, until I slowly trailed a livebait behind the boat: result, a 26lb 12oz pike.

Mike and I have both had barb trebles through the bottom of our thumbs in the last two seasons. Always take care, because accidents can happen all too easily with a pike thrashing about at the unhooking stage. Another problem can occur if you have to net a big pike when one of the trebles of the jerk is outside its mouth. The tangle resulting from hooks embedded in the net and a thrashing pike is not good for either party. I always weigh up a situation after playing the pike in close; as it tires, I get a good look at how it is hooked, and then decide how best to land it, whether on the bank or in the boat.

As you will realize, Mike and I love these gravel pits and now alternate between about twelve of them. In doing so, from last Christmas to April of this year we caught thirteen pike over 20lb, a great many doubles and other large catches. Our best catch was 256½lb in a short day.

Bob's Christmas present from Mike included a 'copper'-painted jerkbait. On its first outing Bob had 90lb of pike, topped by this twenty-pounder.

When Mike and I take *Sneaky*, our sturdy little boat (note that in the interests of safety we always wear self-inflating life jackets when afloat), we always cover the entire pit during the day. This is done by drifting across the pit very slowly by drogue, each of us casting out from different sides of the boat. After completing the drift we motor back upwind on the silent electric motor, move over about thirty metres and then drift across again until the whole water is covered.

As the season wore on I increasingly used the copper spoon in my tactics. Heavy spoons of copper (my favourite), as well as silver and gold, gave us good catches, as good as jerks. When I used my Bob Church 12ft 2½lb test piker, coupled with a well filled baitrunner reel of 15lb line, or heavier if braid, I could cast massive distances with these spoons. To be fair, I took great catches on both methods, because the jerks also gave me two twenty-pounders in two successive casts at another pit (21½lb and 20½lb).

Eight pike for 94lb, followed by one for 16½lb, followed by eight fish for another 90lb: these catches from my last three sessions all came on a new copper-coloured jerkbait made by my fishing companion Mike Green. In the last catch I had two twenty-pounders in less than half an hour, the first time I have managed this using artificials. To say Mike and I were on a piking 'roll' was an understatement: we seemed to 'hit the jackpot' just about everywhere we went at that point in time (2005)!

Mike knows I favour his home-made jerks, so he made me a couple of new ones as a Christmas present. One had extra large eyes and was painted copper in colour, and I had to try it out straightaway. (These heavy wood jerks are internally weighted so as to be slow sinkers.) The idea for the copper colour had come about at one of our Northampton Specimen Group meetings, when member Pete Brittain brought up the subject of colour in artificials. Those present agreed that the action of a lure is important, but it is no good at all if the colour is not acceptable.

During the discussion, Pete Brittain maintained that copper was the colour that aroused big pike best of all. He quoted quite a few examples, mostly from experiences of fishing with large spoons. So a couple of days later, Mike decided to try a copper-coloured jerk; for this he returned to the local river, the Great Ouse, and caught six small jack pike to 6lb, but he also landed a beautiful surprise perch of 2½lb.

So to our pike trip: on went the copper jerk, and many a pike later, it has not come off. It seems to wake up the dourest of pike – they cannot resist it. That first trip produced ten pike for me to 17½lb, for a total weight of 94lb. Another trip to a different pit produced just one pike – but at 16½lb I was pleased, because this is a particularly difficult water.

These trips were within two weeks of one another, and Mike Green continued his run when he and Tim Sumner jerk-fished the River Nene. They only had seven pike that day, mainly small specimens, but Mike did manage one excellent fish of 22½lb. I can tell you that pike over 20lb from the Nene are rare, but Tim and Mike have now had four in the last couple of seasons, all caught on jerkbaits and fly.

Along came Christmas Eve. Most good husbands were out shopping, but I'm afraid Mike and I took advantage of the very mild day. Air temperatures were 50°F – similar to a year earlier, when we both caught twenty-pounders. Lightning was to strike twice – but this time it was Mike doing all the photography for me, as my copper jerkbait worked overtime. My pike came in this order: 7½lb, 10½lb, 14½lb, 9lb, 21lb, 20½lb and 7½lb. Mike used the fly for most of the day on this occasion, giving him four fish to 10lb. Like the fine sportsman he is, he was as pleased with my catch as I was.

My method of working the jerk is now showing to be very successful. It is a similar tactic I use when fly fishing for trout with a sunken line: cast, let the jerk sink for five seconds, then jerk, reel, jerk, reel, then pause for three or four seconds. This action is truly like a dying fish in its final moments. Takes usually come during the pause when the lure is seemingly falling lifeless to the bottom. It won't reach the bottom if you work it right; instead it will be engulfed in a pair of giant jaws!

The other noticeable point at which takes occur is just before the lure reaches the side of the boat or bank; I have even had three pike hook themselves by throwing their bodies out of the water and hitting the jerk when it has been lifted several inches above the water!

During December the pike were definitely grouping in the deeper areas of the various pits we fish. My advice is to keep on the move, whether drifting across the pit in a boat, or just casting and walking a few yards around the bank. Sooner or later you will find a group of pike, and then you can stay a bit longer in a bid to tempt one of the larger females.

It is important to handle pike sensitively. These fish are fragile, as most of us appreciate nowadays, and bad handling and ignorance soon leads to the demise of a good pike fishery; it only takes one ignorant or careless pike angler to ruin a pike fishery for everyone else. With regard to this, Mike told me of an incident he was involved in a short while back: an angler was playing what was obviously a big pike, with his companion looking on. The fish, a twenty-one-pounder, was eventually landed, but both men were nervous of touching it, and froze at the idea of having

to unhook it. It was fortunate for the pike that Mike was there to handle it and take care of its general welfare.

I use a Shimano combined unhooking mat and weigh sling. This is a necessity to prevent damage. I also have a large soft-meshed retaining net where the fish can be given a rest after the stress of landing and unhooking it. After a short rest you can quickly weigh and take your photograph before returning the fish to the water.

There is another potential hazard for both angler and pike during the unhooking process, particularly when lure fishing. After playing the pike, make sure you get a good look at the position of any treble hooks. There is no risk if they are all inside the pike's jaws, because you will be able to net the fish without any concern about loose trebles. If, however, there are trebles outside the pike's jaws, then you could have trouble if you use a net: many pike twist, crocodile-like, when they are in the net, and a loose hook invariably embeds itself in the net mesh. The best way is to land any such fish carefully (and I stress 'carefully') by hand. Make sure that it is played out, and use a glove if in doubt – you don't want a treble in your finger. A head-thrashing movement from a big pike can leave you hooked in the hand with one treble while the other is inside a lively pike's mouth. That can sting a bit!

In my opinion, the presence of big pike in any water is definitely a bonus – even a big carp water. Why? Because the slower-moving, big old fish keep the little jack pike population down. I've seen them on early mornings, in summer, slowly creeping around the shallows and searching out small pike. This is the type of water Mike Green and I have been selecting to fish.

I have used all kinds of spinners, spoons and plugs for pike over the years, and I have caught many big pike on the fly, including twenty-pounders from Grafham

At 22lb 2oz, Bob caught this pike on a big copper spoon.

in the early seventies. However, it wasn't until I had a couple of sessions with Mike that I realized just how deadly artificials can be in the right hands. Up until two years ago I would invariably use natural baits such as roach or bream; but I am not bothered now, because I know I can catch big pike in good numbers throughout the winter. To be honest, all three methods have worked magnificently for us. We have now caught thirteen pike of 20lb in the 2003 season, and Mike has had eight to 29lb, and myself five to 25½lb.

So how did I manage to get on such good form again in the winter of 2004? Fishing with Mike is virtually enough, as he is so clinically good at jerk and fly fishing. However, once again I have to thank the Northampton Specimen Group member, Pete Brittain, who argued the case for copper-coloured lures in the pre-Christmas trip. Pete had arrived at his opinion about copper being the best colour purely by fishing with a big copper spoon. Probably I have more tackle than some shops, however, I didn't own a single

34

copper spoon. So after a quick call to Phil Griffiths, the Coventry lure dealer, I had three good samples sent to me the next day, one silver, one gold and one copper. They were quite heavy, and therefore well suited to long-range casting, allowing me to search more water. At the time Mike was in New Zealand; on his return I wanted to surprise him by taking him to a 40-acre lake, a mature gravel pit that I had not fished for twenty years! I sensed it would be good because, as we have found so many times, neglected pike waters do fish well.

On about the second or third cast I lost a big double at the net on a 5in Blair spoon: this is silver on the outside and copper on the inside. Nothing much else happened, though: I had another couple of hits, and Mike boated two pike on the fly, one a low double, which raised our confidence.

It was now 1pm, and we moved to yet another position. We were drifting slowly with the Bob Church drogue out and I decided to try my new copper spoon. I put in a really long cast and had a follow from a big fish on the retrieve. Something hit the lure on the next cast, but it wasn't hooked. The next cast produced a 22lb 2oz pike, my first fish to the copper spoon. We went to the shore to photograph and return this near-perfect pike. We returned to fish the same spot, and on the first cast, a 21½lb fish came aboard. Whilst I was unhooking it, Mike said 'I'm in!' and quickly boated a 19½-pounder. We temporarily put these in one of my new, large keeper sacks, the reason for this being that we didn't want to waste time photographing them as these feeding spells often only last for short periods. I cast out the copper spoon again, and landed another pike weighing 17½lb. I was enjoying this!

Eventually we took the fish to the bank to get the perfect photograph amongst the daffodils. While Mike set up the camera

In the last few days of the 2005/2006 season I hit the jackpot while fishing at Ravensthorpe Reservoir, when I caught this superb 30lb 8oz pike on fly rod tackle.

for the photos, I carried the three pike, totalling over 60lb, up the sloping bank. In doing so I felt my old sciatic back injury go into a spasm. This time the pike had the last laugh!

I did manage to see the day out, however, and as you will see, it ended up a bit special. My final tally was ten pike, nine of which were doubles. Mike added to this with fish of 19½lb, 13lb and 12lb on copper jerks, plus 14lb, 13lb, 10½lb and 8lb on the fly. In addition he had a couple of fish on a copper spoon. This resulted in a combined catch of 256½lb. Not bad for a couple of old fellows!

2. A History of Pike Angling

by Barrie Rickards

The story of pike angling in this country is as long as the story of angling, as least as far as the written word is concerned. The first book on angling was written by Dame Julian Berners, and in the 1496 edition the section on angling includes a brief account of pike angling. It is a surprising account too, hinting at a lot of pike angling development earlier in that century, if not earlier still. Here is a list of techniques in that book: sunken float rig; threaded trace; attractor smells; free line rigs; and, possibly, ledgered baits, static deadbaits and herring deadbaits. Now, doesn't that list seem surprisingly modern?

Of course, the actual details of the technique are not always clear, and, given the brevity of the text, that is hardly surprising. So we cannot be sure that when talking about the use of herrings for pike on Morton's Leam (near Peterborough) she was advocating static deadbait. After all, in the past, as we shall see, deadbaits were usually fished in mobile fashion. However, if you have spent much time yourself working a herring deadbait, either free-lined or beneath a float, then you will have fished it statically at least whilst you had a coffee, or lunch. I have no doubt myself that static herring deadbaits were in use for pike before 1496, though the literature does not prove it.

In the table at the end of the chapter you will find a summary of pike angling discoveries, plotted through time and in relation to a series of books by the great innovators in pike angling, notably, and in order, Nobbes (1682), Pennel (1865), Bickerdyke (1888), Jardine (1896), Senior (1900), Martin (1907), Spence (1928), Spencer (1936), Hill (1944) and Craig (1951). In the colour plate section you will find photographs of tackle and equipment, including early floats, and reels used prior to the 1950s, as well as images of more modern equipment.

There are two other factors to mention briefly before I get on to the detailed history. The first is Isaac Walton, whose *The Compleat Angler* was published in 1577, about eighty years after Berners; yet it is the least convincing part of Walton. Whereas much of Walton is a superb evocation of angling, his writing on pike has a very second-hand, mythical slant to it. However, he was the first to mention several concepts, namely spun deadbaits, 'walking' baits, gorge fishing, and sink-and-draw fishing. He was also the first to describe line clips. At some time in those eighty years or so, some new ideas arose and Walton recorded them after a fashion. Similar matters are covered in *The Arte of Angling* published at about the same time as *The Compleat Angler*. From this period to Robert Nobbes (1682), the first and great piking innovator, is more than a hundred years, when nothing new seems to have been recorded.

The second factor to mention is the astonishing period in piking that followed

Fenland dawn.

World War II, when nothing less than a revolution took place in the 1950s. This is true of angling as a whole, not least because of Richard Walker and colleagues (and it is also true of many other spheres of human activity). If you examine the table again, it is obvious that this piking revolution did not involve the actual discovery of techniques – for the most part that happened a long time earlier. In fact, if you look at the innovations of Hill and Craig, the last two on our list, they look singularly unimpressive. What happened was the growth of a whole new philosophy of piking, coupled with sophisticated refinements of techniques and tackle. In the text below I plan to show how these techniques, and the philosophy, developed and resulted in far better pike catches than ever before in history, together with seriously improved conservational understanding. The perception of pike, as, at best, the poor man's salmon or, at worst, vermin, would change so that its rôle both as a sport fish and as a vital cog in the ecological machinery would be better appreciated.

It all began with Norman Hill and Thurlow Craig. Hill was the first of the modern pike anglers, but a man who for some reason completely missed the efficacy of static deadbaiting; and Craig was the father of modern lure fishing.

FLOATS AND LIVEBAITING

Youngsters coming into pike angling today will have seen a huge range of well-designed pike floats in tackle shops and catalogues, but may not have seen much in use because ledgering without floats is so commonly practised, at least for deadbait fishing. Older anglers will remember that all bait fishing in the 1950s was float fishing, usually by means of a *Fishing Gazette* float, a bulbous monstrosity, incorrectly streamlined, and with a slit down one side which harboured (sometimes) a peg that supposedly fixed it to the line. In addition there would be one or more pilot floats, smaller floats set on the line above the main float, the purpose of which was to help keep the main line afloat, and also to tell you where the pike was going once it had submerged the main 'bung' (as it became known).

This form of piking went back a long way, it was totally ingrained in the sport, traditional, and no one thought of doing anything else. The bait, usually a live fish, was suspended about three feet below the 'bung', whatever the depth of water. I fished like this for a year or two, and then I began to think.

Floats for piking have been in use since the time of Berners, and she had a sunken float rig. However, the arrangement was unusual. About one yard from the bait would be a lead, and the float was placed midway between bait and lead. In this position, or if the float were nearer the lead, then the herring would fish as a static deadbait on the bottom. If the float were nearer the bait, then the result might be a form of pop-up. This last seems unlikely because one effect, for certain, would be that the herring would slowly swing inwards so that it was directly beneath the float and therefore at risk of tangling the line – unless the float was small, in which case no pop-up effect could occur, and the function of the float seems pointless. The lead, of course, would function almost as the modern carp angler's back lead! It's a puzzle, but it's the earliest record of a float in use (1496, or possibly 1420; see Rickards and Bannister, 1991, p.xi). Nobbes also fished occasionally in Berners' way, but he also fails to explain why the float was between bait and lead.

Returning now to the *Fishing Gazette* float, for that is what leads us into the twentieth century, it seems to have been mentioned first of all by Bickerdyke (1888) in one of the great books *Angling for Pike*. Bickerdyke liked the F.G. 'bung' for exactly the same reason that anglers in the 1960s rejected it, namely its capacity to fall off the line at the slightest provocation. Of course, with silk, flax and cotton line – and I have some 1940s and 1950s experience of cotton lines – the float would have had less of a tendency to fall off the line, but with nylon monofil becoming widely available in the 1950s, the float proved to be useless.

There was more to it than that. Firstly, the hydrodynamics were all wrong, in that the pointed end of the float should have been pointing upwards, rather than into the water: a streamlined shape leads the bulbous side into the medium, as does the leading edge of an aeroplane wing. Secondly, anglers such as those of us fishing in the Fens were beginning to fish deep water and needed a sliding float to facilitate casting. Other anglers, such as Dave Steuart on the Kentish gravel pits, were also devising rigs that needed a sliding float. Before that Norman Hill, in his terrific piking book published in 1940, had worked out that sunken floats in some circumstances and sliding floats in others were really necessary in piking. Somehow Hill's accounts were lost until the 1960s, when they resurfaced; today they dominate angling where floats are used.

In the Fens we moved quickly from inverted, converted slider FG floats to using pilot floats on their own, because they are smaller and give less resistance. We worked a good bead and stop-knot system so that we could fish at any depth. We took our lead from Dave Steuart and fished sliding float paternoster and sunken float paternoster, or we laid on with the float set slightly over-depth. It was the work of a moment to change to free-drifting or free-swimming rigs, so that it really did have the merits of flexibility, something one could hardly argue for the previous traditional outfits. Paternoster rigs (minus floats) came in with Bickerdyke, but do not seem to have been much used in piking until the development of the float paternoster by Hill and Steuart.

One other float was in use in the early 1960s, and this was the dumbbell float used by Dennis Pye in the Broads. This consisted of two spherical floats on a single stem. The arrangement greatly increases the resistance, which was part of the scheme: a shallow-fished, large livebait pulled against the float and could be worked in any direction on the shallow Broads waters. It did not catch on to any great extent because it is not of wide applicability, but it certainly works in the right place. By the 1980s a big range of excellently designed floats was available to keen pikers, and this range included dumbbell floats and 'pilot' floats, as well as carefully (and correctly) streamlined floats, cigar-shaped floats, and so on. Those of us who had always made our own floats found ourselves well catered for.

When we spread the use of float-fished paternoster rigs in the 1960s, through teach-ins and lectures as well as spectacular catches, we emphasized at the time the use of small paternoster leads. In fact we

Barrie with his bait-fishing set-up on the River Delph.

used single swan shot, no more, and there was a good reason for this – or at least, a reason. Richard Walker, whom all serious anglers followed rather slavishly, had always argued against resistance in fishing, that undue resistance led to dropped runs. Hence in piking, we used the smallest lead we could get away with. We now know that this is all wrong, and through the 1970s and 1980s we found that the size of the lead hardly mattered, and so, for various practical reasons, leads were increased in weight up to 2oz or more, depending on the circumstances. Results improved, if anything, because the tackle fished more efficiently at varied distances and in varied flows.

It is necessary now to look at the rest of the paternoster rig: the hook trace or traces, and the trace wire. Trace wires have been used since earliest times because it was soon realized that pike could bite through silk and flax! The traces up until the 1970s were, however, enormously thick and stiff. Finer traces could be obtained of single strand wire – for example, Alasticum – but these had a tendency to kink on the cast, a fact first noted by Bickerdyke in 1888. Then came cabled wires, plastic-coated wires, Kevlar-coated wires and lastly so-called seven-strand wires and various non-steel wires. The modern angler is superbly served, although I would always aim for a wire that does not turn into a curly strand after one or two pike, which seems to me to be the problem with most seven-strand, extra thin wires. Some of these wires are simply too thin, unnecessarily so.

The hook rig developed in another fascinating field. The earliest anglers often used double hooks, as in the gorge-baiting system, and they used hooks not unlike the modern Bellars' hooks, that is with two singles back to back (though these were set to lie flat against the side of the bait, not

proud of it). Later, treble hooks were used, and Bickerdyke seems to have been the first to use a sliding, upper (Ryder) treble. He objected to the large barbs in use, but it is only since about 1995 that barb sizes have been reduced to a size that is closer to what they should be. Jardine, shortly after, introduced the Jardine snap tackle (we have some originals from that era) that employed either a fixed or a sliding Ryder hook; but even Jardine had to put up with hawser-like wire – nevertheless the snap tackle was born, a really crucial invention in piking: in my own opinion it is probably the best rig ever devised. Used with a sliding Ryder, and today's finer wires and small hooks, it remains incomparable and is suitable for both deadbait and livebait fishing. I use it almost exclusively.

I have experimented with barbless hooks since the 1950s, long before the modern angler started to use them. I did so because of the ridiculous barbs on old snap tackles. After a lot of trial I came to the conclusion that micro barbs were best both for hooking fish, and for the conservation of fish; moreover, I am more than ever convinced that fully barbless hooks are damaging and dangerous for pike (and other fish).

So have we seen a full evolution of hooks and hook rigs? Is there more design to come? I cannot see it at present, and most certainly we must get away from stainless-steel hooks because if they are lost in pike they will neither rust nor respond to the acids in a pike's gut. There may also be possible development with single hook rigs, which I have also used extensively for over forty years. However, at the moment we may be at a developmental standstill.

Today there is an increasing tendency to use not only a Jardine rig, but above it, a so-called upper trace, this prevents backlash occurring in either deadbaiting or livebaiting, in which the baited hooks catch on the line above the bottom trace. If a backlash does occur it presents wire to wire, and in the event of a take the pike cannot bite through. Upper traces are a godsend, and all anglers should use them for all bait fishing. Nobbes first used them, so it takes a long time for some good ideas to catch on!

I mentioned gorge fishing above. Anglers themselves outlawed this practice, by which the live fish was threaded on to the trace, in the first part of the twentieth century, although Bickerdyke had condemned it long before. Its demise came when anglers began to return pike to the water, rather than kill them for the pot.

Drifter floats first appeared with Spencer just before World War II, which event probably drove the technique from anglers' minds! In the 1960s it began again with various designs that more or less worked. Someone made a vane rather like that on a throwing dart. I tried these myself and didn't think they worked too well, certainly not as well as Spencer's trimmed swan feather. I remember John Sidley trying drifters, and a specimen group called the Coventry Circus Group in the 1970s, but only two designs seemed to work well: one was a single vane devised by Colin Dyson – I still have mine – and the other, superbly successful, was the single vane system devised by Eddie Turner. This last one seems to have superseded all others, it is widely available, and it really does transport baits a considerable distance once you catch the wind. So once again we have serious development, post-war, of an idea, which had an earlier birth.

In a similar category are ballooning baits, or using bait boats, although these are not necessarily aids to float fishing as they can, and often are, used for ledgering without floats. Each of these is a method of the 1980s onwards, and seems to have no prior history that I can discover. So they really are fully a part of the post-war

revolution. The balloon rig is not particularly complex, requiring only a paper clip attached to a trace swivel. The paper clip holds the balloon knot with just enough tension to allow the angler to strike it off once it has reached the requisite range. Bait boats have a similar arrangement to release the tackle from the mother ship, which is then returned to port!

RODS, REELS AND LINES

I can only give a brief run-down of rods and reels because it really is a vast subject, even when one restricts oneself to only pike and piking. The earliest anglers of the Berners, Walton, Nobbes and Pennel eras either did not use reels, or they had a crude winding horn (or finger) around which the line was coiled. A few reels may have been in use in Pennel's time because he wrote '… not a few have adopted it …', referring to a form of reel.

From Bickerdyke onwards reels of some kind were in use, probably having been 'pinched' from game fishing. Mostly these would have been Nottingham-style reels, including the starback. I used these as a boy, when I graduated from the cheap Bakelite winches, and learned to cast direct from the reel when piking. What is interesting is that Bickerdyke invented the line guard on the Nottingham reel, but it was positioned on the wrong side of the reel for modern anglers. I have one today exactly like that, set up for a left-handed angler. Pennel, Bickerdyke's predecessor as it were, actually had things correct, with the rod in the right hand for a right-handed angler, drawing the line in with his left. He would not have approved of the Bickerdyke line-guard position. That error stayed with us until well into the twentieth century. Of course, most fixed-spool reels, which superseded centrepins in coarse angling, were also set up for left-handed anglers until Richard Walker persuaded angling that that was wrong.

There is nothing wrong with Nottingham reels except that they are rather heavy. Eventually they were replaced by lightweight centrepins, for those who could afford them, and some are still used today by those who like them. I have caught many pike on both reels, and will probably continue to do so at intervals. The arrival of the fixed spool really transformed piking, allowing easy and distance casting of relatively light tackle. In the 1950s fixed-spool reels were relatively crude, some with half bale arm pick-ups (a flying spike!), and many with poor line lay or poor line capacity. Some pricier reels were around, such as the Felton Crosswind, and there were others just fading into the background when I began serious piking.

Intrepid did a reel with a roller bearing in the pick-up, something Richard Walker had pressed for, and now such rollers are universal. Then there was the Mitchel range of excellent reels, all available in left-hand wind; I have several of these and still use them today. Of course the reel is not of prime importance in piking (but see the section on lure fishing below), and even the most beautiful and modern Shimanos are not fundamentally different from earlier fixed-spool reels. Even the bait-runner facility is more useful in carp fishing than it is in pike fishing.

Rods, by contrast, are almost as important as lines. Early rods were of beech, hickory or bamboo, and they were heavy. Even in the first half of the twentieth century pike rods really were like billiard cues (I suspect that that is exactly what some were!) made of stiff whole cane or greenheart. Cheaper rods might have lancewood as a top piece; more expensive rods would be, at least in part, of built (split) cane. I have examples of these rods. Some split-cane rods were very, very heavy and grossly overpowered for the job.

Barrie's first twenty, on ledgered livebait.

The real revolution in rods, brief though it was, came with the introduction of fibre-glass rods in the 1960s. The first ones were poor, of solid glass, indestructible ... but aesthetically hopeless. The hollow glass rods made by people such as Sportex, Davenport and Fordham, and Olivers were excellent; I have several of each, and still use them. It was at this time that rod length increased as weight per unit length decreased, and 11ft rods quickly superseded 10ft rods. Furthermore something else happened at this time, namely the introduction of fast and slow tapers, the so-called tip-action and through-action rods. I still feel that the latter are better for casting large deadbaits a long way, and the former for firing small baits and big leads a long way.

These concept rods stayed with us into the carbon-fibre and carbon-composite rods of the late 1970s – still with us today, of course. The compound taper became more useful in carbon rods (as it had been in split-cane rods, though not in piking split-cane rods); and the end of the glass era – little more than ten years, really – also saw a widespread appreciation of rod test curves. That, too, is still with us: the test curve of a rod is the pull required to pull the rod tip region around so that it is normal to the butt piece (which is fixed during the test). Thus a powerful pike rod has a test curve of about 3lb; much more, and it becomes overgunned, whereas 2¼lb is a little on the light side. Trial and error by pike anglers reached these conclusions. Strangely, the more fragile material carbon is actually more forgiving when it comes to test curve abuse: so if the ideal test curve indicates, say, a 15lb bs line, then monofil of 10–12lb bs can be used safely. It also means that in terms of modern braid lines a much greater bs can be used, the diameter being roughly the same.

I have seen enormous improvements in lines since I began piking in the 1940s. I began with cotton lines for a couple of years before the first monofil nylon lines became available. Cotton, of course, connected me to the era of silk and flax, which went back to the fifteenth century! My first nylon line was a 15lb bs Racine Tortue in green. It was stiff and it was thick, but it did not get into such unpleasant tangles as cotton, and it didn't rot. Well, not exactly. Nylon lines gradually got thinner, more supple, often in pike-friendly colours, and we all had our favourite brands. My favourites for years were Platil and Maxima, both still around today.

Nylon lines did have one problem, in that continued exposure to the sun caused them to lose their breaking strain quite literally overnight. This seemed an especial risk if you had 'pulled for a break' on a snag the previous day. What it did mean was that every time you tied a knot you had to give it an extra yank just to be sure of it. This never happened to Platil in my experience, and only rarely to Maxima. Modern nylon rarely seems to have this defect, and there is now a huge range of high quality lines available. I have never seen the need for a non-stretch nylon, so have avoided these brands, partly because I think they are pre-stretched in some cases and too small a diameter for their claimed bs. Too fine a line, whatever its bs, is not a good feeling in piking.

Just as we reached the stage in the early 1990s of very high quality nylon, so braid came along and partially replaced it. Braid is excellent, and I use it regularly, especially where I need a floating line – though it's worth remembering that in piking a floating line may sometimes be a disadvantage. Braids have been a great success in many aspects of lure fishing. They are particularly good at 'feeling' a take, or a snag – something not really necessary in bait fishing, perhaps.

Barrie with a twenty-seven-pounder, part of the catch in Nottinghamshire with Colin Dyson.

What next in lines? Certainly, high quality nylon and braid will be with us some time. There was a move afoot by some people to turn anglers towards biodegradable line, but I have to say that that seems a nonsense. If it becomes biodegradable during fishing then that is one damaged fish too many.

So despite all the hiccups in the past with rods, reels and lines, and all the efforts of the specialist anglers to avoid various pitfalls – bad design of rod, for example – I doubt if any angler today would do other than applaud the range of rods, reels and lines available. In the 1950s we knew that very little was right: now it almost seems like an evolutionary pinnacle.

LEDGERED BAITS AND FREELINE BAITS

I shall not say much about this technique. Ledgering of deadbaits without a float is very widespread today, possibly too widespread. Increasingly, and very properly, uptraces are in use to prevent backlash and bite-off, and special rigs to attach leads are incorporated. These latter, in the event of a pike breaking the reel line, allow the lead to come free of the tackle and there is then no danger of a tethered fish. Bite indications are usually very adequate, with a combination of buzzer and drop-back indicator giving an early indication of a pick-up.

These developments came about in the 1990s – at least in their complete manifestation. Ledgering itself goes back to Berners and Walton, was toyed with by Nobbes and Pennel, used enthusiastically at times by Bickerdyke, but thereafter rather faded away. When I began piking, ledgering baits seemed unheard of, and I caused a few minor sensations when I introduced it, with livebaits particularly, in the 1950s and early 1960s. I'm not saying it was never done, but I certainly never saw, nor read of it; everyone used a *Fishing Gazette* 'bung'. But my results in East Yorkshire, and again in the Fens, were so good that others began picking up on it, and I dealt with it at some length in my book *Fishing for Big Pike*. Now the technique is widely used, but not usually with livebaits: a strange twist.

What we did find, on some waters, was that ledgered baits produced far more takes than float-fished baits. In one case this may have been because the pike in a hotspot had become wary of floats and floating lines: if they can wise up to lures in a matter of weeks, this is not such a daft idea as it sounds on first reading. Other waters where the method was more successful were actually rather deep waters, so spooking of pike could hardly apply. It may be that the method really does get the bait down to where pike often are much of the time, namely hugging the bottom. A lot of modern ledgering with deadbaits has probably evolved directly from carp fishing, rather than pike fishing. All the summer carper has to do in winter is change his hooklink for a wire trace or two and add a fish bait! It can be a bit unthinking, but it works.

Freelining a bait, dead or live, seemed a good idea to me in the 1950s – after all, it followed Walker's dictum for carp fishing: anything on the line bar a bait was an evil encumbrance. I introduced it in East and West Yorkshire and then to the Fens, and it was as good a technique as ledgering with a lead! The strange thing I found was that false bites were rare with livebaits, and deep-hooked fish were rare to both dead and lives. However, you can't cast as far or as precisely, so presumably that is why the method is out of favour today. Historically it goes right back to Berners and Walton, though it hasn't been used much since.

DEADBAITING

I shall try to constrain myself in this section because it is an area of piking in which I have taken a longstanding interest, and static deadbaiting for pike is one of my favourite ways of fishing, as befits a lazy soul. Deadbaiting began with Berners, and her exposition of the technique is more or less clear. Others such as Pennel, Jardine, Senior and Spence dabbled at deadbaiting, but not in what has become the standard static deadbaiting method. I think they, and certainly Hill, thought that the deadbait, usually a herring, had to be on the move to attract pike. More of this later, but for the present let's deal with the static technique.

Hill completely missed static deadbaiting as a technique, which was quite amazing given all his other discoveries. So there was a very considerable time gap when the method was completely missing from the anglers' repertoire of piking. When I was a boy, static deadbaiting was quite unheard of: only livebaiting and spinning were done. Then in the 1950s Fred J. Taylor and some colleagues began catching good pike on static deadbaits, including herrings, and publicized their results. At the same time Bill Giles and Reg Sandys were using static deadbaits very successfully in Norfolk, and passing on their results by word of mouth. The two techniques were actually rather different. Bill Giles fished his deadbaits tail downwards, so that on the retrieve they would come back head first: he wobbled them back slowly and caught good pike doing this. Fred J. fished the opposite way round, much as we do today, in fact. Most of us followed Fred J.

The actual techniques used were rather crude in terms of hook size, hook arrangement and bite detection. Deep-hooked fish resulted fairly frequently, and this led, belatedly one could argue, to having static deadbaiting banned. The protagonist was the late Konrad Voss Bark, famous as a game angler but rather ignorant of piking, so it seemed to me. Anyway, deadbaiting had moved on and deep-hooked fish had become a rarity by the time Voss Bark wrote against it.

The Taylor rigs, and developments from them, are shown in the first (1971) edition of *Fishing for Big Pike*. The standard Fred J. Taylor rig consisted of what, in effect, was a Jardine snap tackle, but with the trace beyond the hooks threaded through the deadbait emerging at its tail. Both the trebles were towards the front of the deadbait, one stuck in the gill area, the other a little further back, perhaps half way along the bait. The problem with this, we soon found, was that as the pike swallowed a bait head first, the trebles went down the throat quickly, and first! This resulted in too many deep-hooked fish, even for anglers who were very attentive to their floats.

The Dave Steuart rig of the same period comprised two trebles down each flank. The trebles were small, and Dave would strike immediately he got a take. The problem with this rig was that the pike didn't like it. I don't think they were in any way suspicious of all the hooks, but they couldn't get hold of the prey properly and kept ejecting it!

We began to think! We liked Steuart's idea of small hooks, so I changed to sizes 8 and 6 (as opposed to the size 4s, 2s and larger in general use). Ray Webb suggested moving the trebles to the rear of the bait, and as he used only one treble he kept it relatively large and stuck it in the tail end. This all proved much more efficient. At about this time Basil Chilvers started using half baits (for economy!) but with the same hook rig, and, I found out a few years later, Martin Gay had started doing exactly the same down in Essex and Kent. We have never looked back, and this is the rig used today by so many pikers. Half deadbaits were first used by Nobbes (1682), but we didn't know this. One of the good things about a half mackerel or herring is that the bait is never too big, so you can strike quickly in full confidence that the hooks are in. In those days the barbs were unnecessarily rank, so I used to press them down a little so they were little more than a whisker. (I had used barbless hooks in various trials, and found them essentially unsatisfactory. Later I decided that the word 'dangerous' was more accurate.)

Another problem that occurs with the use of static deadbaits, and one which Ray Webb and I experienced fairly early on, was the fact that pike in some circumstances wolfed down the bait very quickly so that deep hooking resulted. A great deal of debate ensued, much of it ill informed. A popular idea for a while was that prebaiting not only attracted pike, but also conditioned them to feed without moving off and so registering a bite. This was wrong, because we found that non-moving takes occurred on waters that had never seen a deadbait. The answer almost certainly is that if the bait is cast into a hotspot or a pike's lair, there is simply no need for it to move off. We have to remember, too, that in those days we were using very light leads, if any at all – slaves to Walkerian principles that we were.

Later, when heavier leads were used, either fixed or free-running, the pike would feel resistance and pull against it, because this is quite natural. You may well ask how this can be quite natural. Well, a pike in nature often feeds in thick weedbeds, and at the time of taking its prey it may well grab weed, too. So it expects to have to pull, and it will keep on pulling until it is free of the encumbrance. Nowadays one hears nothing of pike swallowing-on-the-spot problems, though they must occasionally occur, and anyway bite detection methods are much superior now.

So deadbaiting has come a long way since ancient times, thanks to the pioneering modern efforts of Fred J. Taylor and Bill Giles. Of course, it is not enough to go to a water and chuck out a deadbait and wait. You have to try to work out where the pike might be; or perhaps be quite mobile until you have found a real hotspot. Then keep it to yourself!

You can groundbait. Attracting pike by smell goes right back to Berners, although today it is a more exact science – and yet one still comes across pikers who do not use attractors. At the very least I will throw in chopped-up deadbaits after the day's fishing. I may pre-bait for a long period, but still throw in several pounds of varied fish bits at the end of the day. I cannot understand those anglers who, at the end of a session, chuck their deadbaits in the margins for the gulls to eat. These should go out to where the pike will find them. Get them used to eating a variety of fish in a variety of sizes: in that way they'll not go 'off' a bait because they see too much of it and associate it with capture and recapture.

If you have a cormorant problem on your water, then such a method of groundbaiting or pre-baiting may not work (except whilst fishing) because the cormorants will eat the lot. You can get around

Twenty in the old days.

it in two ways: firstly, mince the fish bits and prepare frozen groundbait balls before going fishing; these will attract pike over a long period, but will not feed the cormorants (or the pike). Secondly, you can put the deadbait chunks in a small wire cage on a rope, which will have exactly the same effect. Neither is as good as being able to use chopped chunks freely thrown in, but it's better than nothing.

You can also use a variety of smells added to a cereal groundbait mix. This has the advantage of attracting both pike and cyprinids, and again, it does not feed the black plague. Another commonly used attractor method, and one I used for many a year, is to put a swimfeeder where the lead normally is, and fill it full of cereal and smells. It certainly works, although it's a bit clumsy and messy!

One of the current deadbaiting techniques that is thoroughly modern and with no hint of a past at all, is the technique of adding attractor colours rather than smell. The deadbait enthusiasts have really taken a leaf out of the lure fishers' book by adding red flashes to a deadbait. The first I ever heard of this myself was back in the 1990s when the Fenland piker Colin Goodge showed me – and gave me – his own plastic red flashers that he used on both dead- and livebaits. He had considerable empirical evidence that they worked

Big twenty, safely held in a big round landing net.

well. Since then, firms have manufactured them, and you can buy packets of them now! This is often the case with specialist anglers' inventions in piking, and I think it would be true to say that both E.T. Tackle and John Roberts Tackle stemmed from their own inventions of new gear.

At about the same time as plastic flashers were being used, so too was the dyeing of baits various colours. Whether or not this is effective, I'm not sure. Logically it should be so, but my own trials have been quite inconclusive. I'm convinced red plastic flashers attract: I'm not yet convinced that dyed baits make much difference.

There is one development in deadbaiting that I do not feel is an advantage at all, and that is the use of hair-rigged deadbaits. Hair rigs were developed in carp fishing to facilitate the hooking of carp, and to some extent to lessen the spooking effect perceived for traditional hooking. Neither of these requirements obtains in pike fishing, and I cannot see any point in going to the lengths of hair-rigging a bait for pike. It seems now to be falling out of favour a little, which hardly surprises me.

I have left until last another modern technique that seems to have little historical past: the fishing of pop-up baits. As far as I can ascertain, these came in in the 1960s when we began to use them in the Fens. I also used rods and polystyrene pieces to make a deadbait stand on its tail on the bottom. My idea was that this would help spread the smell on any wafting current, increase the visibility, and perhaps assist the pick-up by the pike. It seemed to work, and it did slowly catch on. Today you can buy shaped balsa rods, and Fox do bright red balls that can be attached to one end of the deadbait to pop it up. Deadbaits can be popped up well off the bottom, or critically balanced, and the bright red balls have the added attraction of visibility. They are so successful that today I wouldn't consider deadbaiting without one of my deadbaits on a Fox pop-up, with or without a Goodge red flasher.

Perhaps as a final point, an interesting aside that epitomizes attitudes to static deadbaiting in the 1950s before the Taylor/Giles discoveries: when I was editing, and partly writing, a French predator book in the 1990s (half a century after the efficacy of deadbaits was discovered in England) the French utterly refused to believe that a pike would pick up a dead fish lying on the bottom. It was a complete myth, they said. The prey had to move through the water to be taken by pike. Just shows you... Possibly this is the right moment to move on to the next section.

Spun Deadbaits and Sink-and-Draw Deadbaits

Sink-and-draw deadbaiting is the earlier of the two systems, coming in with Berners, Walton and Nobbes, especially the latter two. Nobbes specialized in the method, considering it superior to, and more conservation-like than other methods (that is, it killed fewer pike!). The term used in those days was trolling, which came to have a quite different meaning in the twentieth century (*see* the section later on trolling). Sink-and-draw was also used by Pennel and Bickerdyke, but not much after that, and not at all by Jardine, until the 1960s onwards. From this time it has had a small and enthusiastic, but sporadic following. The best writing I have come across on this subject is that of Jim Gibbinson who, in one of his enthusiastic phases, went into it very carefully. This coincided with a time when Ray Webb and I were also investigating the method, and we took a short cut by simply following Jim's lead!

As with so many matters, J.G. worked things out very thoroughly. The strange thing was that I personally did not find it as rewarding as static deadbaiting, so I gave it up, as did Ray. It's a very fiddly way of fishing, so much so that it is preferable to make up a dozen baits, plus hooks, and deep freeze them before going out for a day's piking. I also found it a cold way of fishing, and as I prefer to be static and warm rather than mobile and cold, and as the results didn't seem all that spectacular, I consigned the method to history. Furthermore I have a suspicion that this is just the reason why the method has not really caught on. After all, you have to have a bait that is firm enough to cast and recast – a sprat, say – or one that has been gutted and stitched up again to the same end. Very fiddly, I found it.

Spun deadbaits really come in with Pennel, and spinning flights of that era are still available because salmon anglers use them! Pike anglers rarely do, although the technique was in vogue in Martin's time, and again in the first half of the twentieth century. I have tried this technique in the past, using mostly fresh sprats or preserved sprats (I still have some with a thick lacquer coating!), and it is both enjoyable and effective. I gave it up in the end because I became an avid artificial lure angler and, once again, the fiddly goings-on with spinning flights put me off. Both wobbled deadbaiting and the spinning of deadbaits are ancient techniques that stutter on into the twenty-first century, but they haven't evolved much, and nor are they likely to. It would be nice to be wrong about this.

UNHOOKING AND HANDLING PIKE

Until now I have been considering pike angling from the point of view of using natural baits, because that has the longest history, is in a sense natural from the pike's point of view, and is a facet of piking that has shown considerable evolution over the centuries, as I hope I have shown. Before going on to look at the evolution of lure fishing I want to pause for a time to discuss the matter of unhooking pike and the handling of them, because this is an area where there has been enormous change since the 1950s, far more than at any time previous to that. What is more, I was personally right at the centre of the debate, so know exactly what happened.

To set the scene and also effect a contrast, I need to begin at the beginning. Before Pennel, anglers grasped the pike by its eye sockets and lifted; Pennel, however, more or less put an end to that. Before 1950, pike anglers used a gaff to land their fish, and most fish were killed for the pot. There was some development of the gaff in the 1950s with Richard Walker suggesting a better bend shape than the round bend gaffs used by salmon anglers. I had one made myself to Walker's design, but as the gaff in pike fishing was simply slid under the jaw of the pike (unlike salmon fishing, where it was stuck in the flank of the fish) I couldn't see that the new design was any better than the old. Both were very inefficient. One could attribute to Walker the demise of the gaff in pike fishing, because of the development of the landing net in carp fishing. Here was a tool with the capacity to engulf pike without having to fiddle about attempting to slide a gaff into its jaws without sticking the point in the fish.

Nets in the 1950s were very small unless you went to the trouble to build a big one. I did it, in 1964, by making a 30in (76cm) diameter loop of black mild steel (¼in/6mm) and simply hanging the big net on that. Big salmon nets were available; the hoop had three hinges so it folded away easily. I then had a ⅜in (9mm) BSF bolt welded on a tiny ring, and the landing net handle screwed easily on to that. I use exactly the same thing today, in a slightly larger diameter and with lighter material in the loop. They do look enormous, and they certainly turned the heads of a few experienced pike anglers when they saw it on the bank. But one week after making it I landed, easily, a pike of 29lb 10oz. I needed no more justification, and since then six bigger pike have graced the net.

The landing net was a great step forwards, but it must be remembered that nets in the 1960s had knots, and these became illegal, later to be replaced with micromesh nets. Micromesh nets are not pike friendly at all, however: they remove too much slime, and if hooks get caught in them they are the very devil to get out. Anglers made various attempts to get around this problem, but it is a good example of their crazy kind of logic that instead of using a mesh that is pike friendly (stiff material with a larger mesh size), they opted for barbless hooks, or began to practise hand-landing of pike, variously justifying both methods. Thankfully, by the year 2004 a number of good mesh nets were being developed, and I have hopes that pikers in general will see commonsense and move away from micromesh and barbless hooks. All this development would have amazed pre-war anglers because, then, care of the pike didn't matter a great deal except to anglers like Norman Hill and some anglers on the Norfolk Broads.

So you have the pike in the net, preferably on the bank, or grass. What do you do next? Well, until the 1950s, and even today in some quarters, anglers used a gag, a spring-loaded device that forced the pike's jaws apart. (If you remember the days of gas, at the dentists, then you'll have some idea!) The gag, I decided as long ago as the 1950s, was seriously inefficient. Fishing in East Yorkshire I used a tiny gag for small pike and a bigger one for bigger pike, but you still had to open the jaws a little to get

How to carry a bucket of lures for piking.

it in! I also tried small lengths of wood rather than a gag, and, like so many later anglers, I wrapped tape around the points of the gag. Then in about 1957, possibly earlier, I was fiddling with the small gag and a pike of about 2lb. For some reason I lifted the pike up by holding it under the chin, I think to try to remove the mackerel spinner simply by use of forceps. I noticed that its mouth opened slightly and I was able to remove the spinner quite easily.

I never looked back. From that day onwards the gag was left at home, and I unhooked all pike by the new method. If the jaws didn't open of their own accord, I pushed them gently with one finger and they did so. I demonstrated this to many anglers, because they always crowd around when you have a pike. Later I gave teach-ins and lectures, took photographs, and 'sold' the method to almost everybody (except Ray Webb, who stuck firmly to his

Good, but old, twenty. It subsequently recovered and put on several more pounds.

gag). By the mid-1960s many anglers were on the technique, and Ryan Tingay improved it by using a cloth on the fish-holding hand so that not even scratches resulted. Then some of us replaced the cloth with a soft glove, and before the 1970s the technique we now use was up and running. With larger fish we tended only to lift the head off the ground, often with the fish lying on its back. It is of interest that for several hundred years nobody spotted this technique until a young lad fishing small lakes – actually railway borrow pits – stumbled on it.

Some other thoroughly modern improvements have been effected in recent years. In post-war times keepnets were widely used, and we used them for retaining pike, too. Many anglers resisted the use of keepnets, not because they feared for the pike's health, but because they thought the pike would eat its way out! I kid you not. Some of us were of the opinion that returning a pike immediately to your swim would affect other pike in the swim, just as returning a perch undoubtedly removes the shoal in many instances. Later we couldn't be bothered to retain them, so returned them. From the point of view of on-going catches on the day I'm still not sure that returning them immediately is a good idea.

The keepnet was replaced by the keep-sack, one for each pike. This was much kinder on the pike, and it enabled anglers to get the camera ready without troubling the pike. One other thing happened to do with handling on the banks, and that concerned the principles of weighing. Until the last war, because most pike were killed, they would be weighed on the kitchen scales if small, and on 'pig scales' if large – if, that is, they were weighed at all. But as the specimen hunting movement burgeoned, including pikers, pike were weighed at the waterside before being returned alive.

This particular movement, of returning pike alive, had begun with Norman Hill before the war, but only began to gain ground in the 1950s. My own mentor, when I was a child, was an angler called Mike O'Donnell (now a successful fish farmer in North Yorkshire). He returned all his pike carefully, but he told me that he knew of no other angler who did so, outside his own family. Another famous northern angler, Dug Taylor, was involved in a rough encounter when he attempted to prevent a gang of match anglers slaughter some pike they had caught on the Yorkshire Ouse; but gradually during the 1950s the message spread that it was better for fisheries for pike to be returned, and, of course, it was better for the pike population.

The actual weighing was, by today's standards, rather crude. Because we unhooked pike efficiently by lifting them under the chin, we decided to weigh them quickly the same way; so the hook of the balance replaced the finger, and the weighing was carried out quickly. In fact, in my own view this is not really as bad a method as the young modern angler believes, but it does have one serious drawback in inexperienced hands, in that if the pike leaps, then it can crash to the ground. Today's younger anglers invented not only the unhooking mat, most useful if there is no soft grass, but also the soft weighing sling that cradles the fish without risk. It takes a little longer but is much more efficient than chin-weighing.

The only downside to modern practices is that, often, far too long is taken photographing or filming fish before they are returned. With two anglers present there is no problem because one can photograph whilst the other deals with the unhooking and weighing (and posing) but an angler on his own needs to prepare the camera in advance or, alternatively, put the fish in a keepsack for a time whilst equipment and pose is prepared. If in doubt, don't bother! Some of the banks I fish today make any photography virtually impossible if you are alone. The fish comes first: that is the modern motto.

In summary, it is rather difficult to see where improvements can now be made to landing and handling pike. In the near future there will be an improvement to net materials, and I should like to see more sense in the style of the landing-net rim used; triangular nets are really unsuitable for pike fishing, and without any doubt so is micromesh netting. I would also like to see a decline in hand-landing: I have done a lot of it, so I do know what I'm talking about. It is not a good way to teach new pikers. Although improvements could be made in the philosophical and scientific approaches to pike stock conservation, I shall deal with that matter later in this section.

ARTIFICIAL BAITS

Trolling

The modern term 'trolling' is really a misnomer, as was pointed out by Fred Buller many years ago. Trolling à la Walton to Bickerdyke really meant what today we would call sink-and-draw. The art of pulling an artificial lure behind a boat should really be termed 'trailing', but the word 'trolling' is now too entrenched in the literature to make it worthwhile changing. Artificial baits were only just gaining ground in Pennel's time (1865), but by Bickerdyke's era they were well advanced, and Bickerdyke himself writes authoritatively about them. Of course, his selection of spoons was abysmally low even by post-war standards, but the expertise was there, for sure. I think that trolling probably preceded casting and retrieving from the bank (spinning), because the latter was difficult at the time, and most serious and leading pike anglers boat-fished. It was also at about this time that British and North American pikers diverged. The North Americans went into lure fishing in a big way, but it was not until the 1980s that the range of lures and techniques was fully available here.

Trolling continued here, initially on the oars, later on the outboard motor. When I trolled in Ireland in the 1960s, most trolling was still done on the oars and I became quite accomplished at it. In the 1980s and 1990s trolling has changed out of all recognition because of sophisticated downrigger systems, equally sophisticated echo sounders, lead-covered lines, wire lines, a huge range of trolling lures, and quite excellent rolling motors. Boats have improved from the traditional heavy, leaky, clinker-built boat of my youth, to custom-built craft. The Americans advanced way ahead of us in their use of boats, as in other aspects of lure fishing, and only infrequently have we adopted their type of boats.

When trolling, the actual techniques are very personal and, moreover, need to be varied greatly on the day. The pike may be shallow or deep, active or sluggish, on one lure or the other. So it is an active game requiring intelligence and action, and not merely a matter of pulling a lure unthinkingly behind a boat. Trolling in the UK is best done in Scotland, the large English lakes, Wales and Northern Ireland, or Eire. It is not easy, and it is sometimes illegal, to troll English rivers and lakes; I have done both, and enjoyed it. I have also been caught! The English trout reservoirs also afford some opportunity to practise the technique, but if I had a choice I'd head for the Republic of Ireland, or I would, if I could find somewhere where they did not rather stupidly slaughter their pike.

Any number of specialist bits of equipment have been developed for keen trollers, including good rod holders that keep the butt of the rods above the gunwales; unhooking mats to lay on the duckboards; good seats, and small cabins; lure containers; and so on. Good watercraft is becoming the norm rather than the exception. What we have in trolling in the UK is now high class and getting better, although not a lot of it evolved here: it was imported piecemeal from the USA from around 1970 onwards. Before that it was primitive – and still is, for me.

Artificials: Lure Fishing

Spinning really began with Pennel in the

Tim Cole with a big twenty from a Fenland drain.

1860s, at least in the UK. Pennel discussed the terms 'trolling' and 'trailing', and may have been responsible for trying to introduce the latter. Trolling he defined as pulling in a bait by hand (thus it fits easily into the manner of sink-and-draw used by Berners, Walton and Nobbes), whereas trailing was what we now call trolling; Pennel also refers to trolling as 'spinning'. Interchanging the two words, and use of the term 'spinning', may have begun at that time. It hasn't changed since, and really refers to the use of spinners, spoons and, later, plugs. Nowadays, and since about the 1980s, we tend to call it lure fishing.

In Bickerdyke's time, the late 1880s, reels were in more widespread use, mostly Nottingham-style centrepins. Lures were becoming more common, and the available types included kidney spoons, early Norwich spoons, Colorado spoons, the Holroyd-Smith spoon, and various spinners. Of course, baits were still used on spinning flights, some of which had 'plastic' or metal vanes such as the Archer, Kilko and Crocodile. The 'plastic' was a form of Perspex or Bakelite.

It was probably at about this time that British and North American lure fishing diverged, the latter to evolve spectacularly with the use of a great range of lures and multiplying reels, whilst the former stayed very primitive indeed in comparison. Thus Jardine is not known for spinning, though he did spin baits (and pointed out that cotton lines soon kinked and twisted if used for this purpose). In fact Jardine's spinners really look like a modification of spinning flights, which is probably what they were. Others were simply the salmon anglers' minnows. At this time the US was developing a big range of floating and diving plugs that were not available in the UK.

In the years that followed spinning was done, but of the great angler/writers (*see* the table at the end of the chapter) only Sidney Spencer exploited spinners to the full, and he was very successful with them – and this was pre-war. Norman Hill did spin, but his son David told me that the pikers of the day did not like the Colorado spoon (one of the most widely available lures!), and certainly they had a bad name in the 1950s and 1960s when I began lure fishing myself. Hill preferred copper and

nickel (Norwich) spoons, and copper bar spoons.

Then post-war we had Thurlow-Craig, famous columnist for the *Sunday Express* (the 'Up Country' column) and author of the classic *Tackle Maker's Delight* and *Spinner's Delight*. He is truly regarded as the father of modern lure fishing in the UK, and in his making of plugs perhaps began the slow merger with US lure anglers, finally completed in the 1990s. Thurlow-Craig made his own lures, some bizarre by modern standards and ideas, but they did work on the Montgomery Canal. He regarded lure fishing as the most sporting method of pike fishing – and this is one of the few thoughts where I part company with him: to me it is the angler who is sporting, or not, rather than the method.

Thurlow-Craig's fishing rods were not perhaps the greatest tools for the task, but he did at least reject converted tank aerials, considering that they should be used only for what they were designed. We agree with that: I didn't mention tank aerials in my review of rod development above, but there was a short period in the early 1960s when they were in use ('pressed into' use might be a better expression for it). I have a tank aerial spinning rod of that vintage: it looks nice, but is totally useless for spinning.

Multiplier reels for piking also came in with Thurlow-Craig, who was an enthusiast. They had been used by salmon anglers for some time, but had not crossed over. However, T-C's enthusiasm did not transfer to any more than a few other enthusiasts, and it was not until the 1990s that they became very popular with British pike anglers, especially lure fishermen. In part this increase in use was down to the burgeoning sport of jerkbait fishing – of which more later.

Multipliers improved gradually from the 1950s, and by the 1990s left-hand-wind models were readily available for right-handed anglers. During the same period they began to incorporate sophisticated magnetic brakes, which prevented over-runs very well, even if they detracted a little from distance. I used to begin by setting the brake to 'mug's setting' and then, as I got used to the reel, unclicked it stop by stop until I could cast all day even without much use of the brake; that and the LHW facility make for very comfortable lure fishing. In general I find multipliers more accurate, and fixed-spool reels better for distance – at least in my lure fishing.

Thurlow-Craig made one strange error of judgement: he decried the range of US lures, and, I suspect, did not really approve of much except home-made gear. We are lucky in that his son, Tony Thurlow-Craig, is still around and able to put us right about his famous father!

When I began lure fishing in the 1950s the choice of lures was small. The main ones I used were mackerel spinners, Veltic barspoons, Colorado and Kidney spoons, the Plucky Bait (now extinct), and metal and quill minnows. There was also a 4in (10cm) jointed wooden plug with double hooks, and a tendency for the wood to swell when it got wet, which cracked off the paint. Even so, it caught pike. In 1957 I bumped into four adult anglers fishing American lures in the small lakes at Easington in East Yorkshire, where I used to catch lots of pike. Their lures were beautiful, but they didn't have a fish all day, whilst I had four. For this reason I dismissed US lures as useless, a mistaken judgement similar to that of Thurlow-Craig. I should have realized that those four adults didn't know the waters, and, if the truth were known, didn't really fish very well. I recall now that they seemed more interested in cigars, drink and lunch.

In the 1960s lure availability improved only slightly, but there was a short-lived lure-fishing revival led by Fred Wagstaffe and Bob Reynolds. The trouble with this particular revival was that bait fishing was really taking off in the UK, especially dead-bait fishing, and I'm never really sure just how much inspiration those two anglers imbued in pikers. The number of lures seemed not to increase at all. What they did do, without question, was hammer home the correct message about US lures – that they worked well and in varied circumstances. It may have been the writings of Fred and Bob that persuaded Ken Latham of Potter Heigham in Norfolk to import thousands of US lures in the late 1960s and early 1970s. His shop was an eye opener, and many of us made the pilgrimage to buy Crazy Crawlers, Creek Chubs and many more with glorious American names, and we learnt to fish them.

Even then the sport did not take off. You could lure-fish the Fens all weekend, as Tim Cole and I often did, perhaps fishing a dozen waters, and you'd rarely see another lure angler. So why, in the 1980s, did a real boom in lure fishing take place, and why is it sustained, seemingly, today? Certainly the availability of an increasing number and variety of lures must have helped. I had a long-running column in *Coarse Fisherman*, and gave monthly lectures, which must have helped. Then came newer anglers such as Charlie Bettell, doing the same thing; and one company, TC Lures, not only imported lures by the thousand, but also demonstrated how well they worked. People working for the same firm founded the Lure Anglers' Club (still going strong), and its magazine certainly helped spread the word, as did the events they organized; but perhaps most of all, anglers slowly realized that you could catch big pike on lures – previously there was a myth insisting that lures only caught small pike. I published an analysis of my own twenty-pounders and found to my surprise that if

Barrie carefully returning a big one.

considered on a rod-per-day basis, which is the only sound statistical method, the number of lure-caught twenties was almost as high as deadbait-caught twenties. I remember one very famous bait angler, Mick Brown, considered that lures could never be as good as baits. He might not be so positive about that now, although I do feel myself that pike go 'off' individual lures much more quickly than they go 'off' baits.

Today's generation of lure anglers includes some very innovative types, such a Dave Kelbrick and Dave Lumb – and plenty more, too. They are keeping the fire stoked up; as, I suspect, is the availability of trout waters, now opening their doors to lure fishing for pike. Add to that the lure-fishing exploitation of Lakeland's big lakes – Windermere, Esthwaite and so on – and the continued success on Loch Lomond, not to mention Ireland, and we may now have a mix that will sustain the lure-fishing boom for many years.

There are successive waves of enthusiasm for particular families of lures. I recall being involved, with Bruce Vaughan, for introducing the spinner-bait boom in the 1980s; Fred J. Taylor had been there before, but the time wasn't right for him. Then we had the crank-bait era; crank baits are simply what Ken Whitehead and I, in our lure-fishing books, referred to as floating/diving plugs. There was also the jerkbait boom, and now we are in the rubber/soft lure boom. All these lure families continue, of course; it simply means that more styles and methods are available, and they'll all come back again in future booms and crazes, I'm sure. What next, is perhaps the question.

In summary, we have come a very long way since 1970, not least because of the antics of people such as Gordon Burton, who have continued to fly the flag well for US lures, US approaches and, as we see in this volume, US and North American

adventures. So the lure range is incomparably better than in the past, more waters are available, more boat fishing (in better boats) is there to be had, and the rods and reels have never been better. It's a healthy situation, and something so modern that it is post the usual 1950s/1960s boom in pike angling in general – even though, as I accept, the roots of good lure fishing go back at least to that time.

FLY FISHING FOR PIKE

Fly fishing for pike is even more recent in its boom development than lure fishing: the Pike Fly Fishing Association was formed only in 2000, but is developing well. Although historically there have been accounts of pike caught on fly, such as the one illustrated by Bickerdyke, it would be wrong to claim a long-standing basis for the sport in Britain.

When I first used a fly myself for pike it was back in the 1960s and 1970s, and it was a rather crude system. I wanted to see if they would work, so I used an ordinary spinning rod, fixed-spool rod, nylon monofil lure and, set some distance up the line, a wooden former as a casting weight. This was threaded on the line, and I used a match to fix it in position. The position was related to the depth. The greatest success I had was on waters that in summer were shallow and weedy. In the autumn I set the former at about 3ft (1m) above the fly. The fly was concocted out of barred jay feathers, perhaps 3in (7.6cm) long, and it was fished on an ordinary 12in (30cm) Alasticum trace. I suppose it was sink-and-draw really, because the fly was allowed to sink after the former had settled, and then the tackle slowly pulled so that the fly rose towards the surface. Then I let it sink again, and repeated the manoeuvre. I caught any number of pike and perch but

Barrie with a big one from a small drain.

nothing big, which may only have reflected the waters being fished; but I became convinced that pike took flies readily. Later, during the reservoir trout-fishing explosion, pike were taken regularly on fly, confirming what I already knew.

During the early phase of the reservoir trout boom, pike were not often targeted as

This pike took half a mackerel with half-digested eel in its craw.

such, but were accidental captures. Nor was the tackle usually man enough for the job. In contrast, today's reservoir trout anglers often target pike and they use strong enough gear: no. 10 rods and reels, a heavy enough leader, and so on. This is the tackle that the Pike Fly Fishers Association recommends because it would be irresponsible to fish for summer pike, at least, with tackle that prolonged the fight unnecessarily.

A trace of wire is absolutely necessary. In deadbait fishing a cabled trace is preferable to single strand, but in fly fishing for pike the opposite is the case; in fact many anglers use piano wire, which makes a short, stiff trace of perhaps 9in (23cm) in length. Some designs, especially by the Dutch angler/artist Ad Sweir, are superb and do not need a link swivel, thus lightening the load at the fly end of the gear.

Flies themselves can be huge, or, as someone said, like a drowning parrot. Pike will take small flies, too, though, so it doesn't pay to get carried away. Once again, Ad Sweir solved some of the problems with very large flies by producing some that barely gained weight when soaked – so they were easier to cast than the proverbial soaked parrot.

I think pike fly fishing is here to stay, and it seems to gain advocates by the week. One can fish deep water, too, of course, as well as employing a number of fly-fishing techniques: some lures, for example, pop up when the retrieve is stopped.

PIKE BAITS

I have already covered some aspects of baits because they are necessarily part and parcel of the earlier sections, so I shall be brief in this section. Livebaits nowadays have to be caught on the water on which the piker is fishing or is about to fish; transporting them is illegal. Small trout are provided on some reservoirs, and this is perhaps the way to go, with the water's owners supplying, at a cost, an appropriate variety of baits. Everyone has his favourite livebaits, and this is mentioned from time to time in ancient texts, too. Apart from small trout, tiny chub make one of the best baits, as do tiny bream and small perch. Others are less robust. In fact, the only change in modern times on the livebaiting front is that anglers today are much more catholic in their tastes, whereas in ancient times the bait was roach or dace, or roach or dace!

In the world of deadbait fishing there have been enormous changes. In the past I suspect it was herring or sprat, or possibly dead coarse fish. The same was true in the 1950s when I started following Fred J. Taylor and Bill Giles; when you look through the old literature it is a surprise to find that Norman Hill used mackerel. In the 1960s no anglers used mackerel, but Peter Wheat on the Hampshire Avon began to use them very successfully at about the same time as one of our colleagues on the Relief Channel. Of course, these would be used whole, which gave striking problems of which Norman Hill was very aware. Once the half bait was 'invented', striking problems disappeared, as did those relating to casting.

The introduction by Neville Fickling of smelt as bait was most important, as was the popularization of sardines by Bill Chillingworth, because it caused anglers to look more widely at different kinds of bait.

No comment.

Eels were used as deadbaits in ancient times, but they were re-invented in the 1980s, and really are a good bait. (They should be obtained from reputable suppliers, rather than risk depleting our waters of eels by taking one's own catches.) Lampreys, too, have been a great success. I must relate a couple of stories to you with respect to smelt and lampreys, which will show you just how important it is to keep an open mind and to try anything. In 1961 and 1962 I used to roach fish on a large lake on the north shore of the Humber estuary, and in that water were countless smelt; we caught many of them. In the same water were crabs, seaweed and codling because of a connection with the Humber – though it never occurred to me to try them for deadbait. A few years later we caught smelt again on the tidal River Ouse in the Fens, and this time we *did* use them for bait. The results, however, did not seem particularly good, so I abandoned the idea!

The lamprey story is even worse. Having caught several large pike on the Relief Channel, with anything up to three lampreys in their throats, I decided it would make a good bait. This was circa 1968. I knew a stream in East Yorkshire with lots of lampreys in it, so I made the journey to see if I could get a tubful. Unbeknown to me, the authorities had, in my absence from the North, built a prison on the banks of the stream, and to cut a long story short I was 'arrested' on its banks and given my marching orders in no uncertain terms. I then lost interest in lampreys as bait. Two missed opportunities there, as anyone piking today will know.

The huge range of sea deadbaits now available to us, plus some freshwater baits (trout, salmon, eels, smelt and pollan), is very important. Other freshwater fish can be used too, of course, but they must be caught on the water, I suspect, even if you

intend freezing them for future use. The important thing on any water is to make sure that the pike see a variety both as bait and as groundbait. Don't get hooked into one bait because you think it's the best: some days you'll find the pike will take any species, whereas on others they'll select smelt, or mackerel, or sprat. As well as deep-frozen baits it pays, in my opinion, to try them fresh from the fishmongers' slab. This is especially important with mackerel, because the oily effect is lost on bait frozen for too long. So I usually have both with me on any trip, the deep-frozen ones for long casting, the fresher ones for close work.

Everything of the last few paragraphs is of the 1990s and 2000s. In the 1960s and 1980s we were relatively unadventurous with our range of deadbaits, even though some of us were trying plaice, cod, haddock and other fish species. I still am. There is a great contrast between how we fish deadbaits now, and how we fished them twenty or more years ago, and a very big contrast with ancient times when I think they were a little unsure of static baits.

MODERN PHILOSOPHIES

When Ray Webb and I wrote *Fishing for Big Pike* (1971), we introduced a whole series of ideas that were regarded as relatively new, if not completely new: feeding patterns, times of day, hotspots and the lair theory, and so on. Others had been thinking along the same lines I think, which is why the book got such a good reception; it marked the time, I think, when the old piking really was past: the *Gazette* bung had gone, rigs were good, static deadbaiting was here, lure fishing was on the move, and anglers everywhere were catching pike. This was not always the case, good catches previously being restricted to the Broads,

Bleak mid-winter in Fenland. Note continued use of drop-off indicators and buzzers (floats are also in use).

Hornsea Mere, Slapton Ley and a few other places. Nor were many anglers involved in success – Dennis Pye, primarily, Bill Giles, Fred Taylor and friends. A lot of the writing in the first half of the twentieth century was little more than paying lip service to the old saws on piking.

If you look back carefully, there were some observations that should have taken off in a big way, but did not .... The same old story, if you will, of many good discoveries. For example, Bickerdyke considered that the best time for pike was from daybreak until 9am. What on earth happened to that fundamental observation? It wasn't heard of again until the legendary Tag Barnes wrote an article in *Angling* claiming that on the Lincolnshire drains, dawn to 9am was the time. People laughed at him, and most certainly, when Ray Webb and I were travelling the country, most pike anglers started the day at 10am or 11am. On the Relief Channel they didn't get a run, and yet had missed the most spectacular fishing earlier that morning, often with several hundred pounds of fish caught.

Feeding patterns, though, did seem to escape all the writers until Ray Webb picked it up in about 1962–63. He noticed that on any one water the pike came on the feed simultaneously, fed for a short while, maybe an hour or two, then stopped, presumably after feeding successfully. On one television programme the producers openly sneered when he told them that filming would be a waste of time until 4pm in the afternoon when the pike would feed, but that is exactly what happened, and Ray landed a 20lb fish for them, the run coming at precisely 4pm. This pattern had been maintained for weeks, so he knew what he was talking about. I and many other anglers thought he was talking nonsense, but over a couple of years we became absolutely convinced as it was

demonstrated over and over again. Today, of course, most serious pikers recognize that whilst every water is unique, each will have its own feeding pattern.

Then there is the matter of hotspots. Although in *Fishing for Big Pike* this was claimed as an innovation, it had, in fact, already been spotted by Peter Wheat fishing in Hampshire; we simply reached the same conclusions at the same time. All the spectacular feeding mentioned above took place in very small areas, repeatedly. We often fished five or six of us, in and either side of our hotspots, and all the fish were caught in the hotspots bar the odd jack or an occasional double. We shared the hotspots, both on a rota and by mixing up rods. The only exceptions were when, conditions being perfect, the pike left the hotspots and fed everywhere; this is when a water seems wholly alive with feeding pike. The next day they'll be back in their hole, and if you get a run at all after such a spree, it will be in the hotspot and nowhere else.

Hotspots like this are few and far between even on big waters, but if you don't find them, sport will be patchy. Certainly they can be overfished and spoilt, but on the other hand, I've been fishing one for twenty-seven years, but never overfishing it, and it still produces the goods. The concept has been criticized from time to time, but never convincingly – though it's good that today's anglers examine it, of course. Some of the old anglers – Bickerdyke again – were aware of what they called 'shoaling', but this was really pre-spawning and spawning gatherings. At such times hotspot occupants will head for the spawning grounds, but they go back again later!

A final point is that most of the hotspots I know, whether on drains, rivers and lakes, have no obvious tie to physical features such as weedbeds, drop-offs, sunken trees, or whatever, but mostly they seem to be in totally 'blank' places. That is not to say that you don't get pike in features, because you do, but they use them as cover when hunting actively, rather than sitting quietly in the bailiwick.

Barometric pressure – and now lunar cycles – is not new in pike angling or, indeed, in angling. It's just that in *Fishing for Big Pike* I made the case for pressure with respect to piking (having first spotted it in tench angling). Game fishermen have known of the effect of barometric pressure for at least two hundred years, so although I'm thoroughly convinced that it's important in piking, historically it is well established. No change there, then. I think the same can be said about warm south-west winds. Everyone now knows that a warm south-west blow after a cool/cold spell or a spell of unsettled weather really does produce results. This was well known in ancient times and probably has been so throughout pike-angling history. We should never ignore its role, although it is, if you like, old hat. The lunar cycle debate is on-going, and the concepts probably are relatively new in piking. I've got an open mind on this one: I feel that the lunar enthusiasts have got it right, but some of them may be over-egging it in detail. I don't have time now to chase this question myself!

Barrie's ancient car (still going strong) and boat (ditto).

The ecology of pike is far better understood today, and, slowly but surely, barbaric practices (and, indeed, time- and money-wasting practices) are dying out. There's the occasional idiotic flutter now and then, and the western Irish still seem to live in the 1800s, but progress is steady. Most people now recognize that big pike (over 10lb) really need to be returned to the water, the consequences of not doing so resulting invariably in a great upsurge of jack pike and increased predation on cyprinids and trout; in short, the bigger pike control their brethren, and are serious cannibals. I know one water where in the late spring there are dozens of jack pike a few inches long (they take spinners regularly), yet by the late autumn they have quite disappeared – down the big pikes' gullets; and I'm sure this is normal.

Even on big trout reservoirs, if the pike are left alone or handled carefully, you have a relatively small population of big pike. And here's a thought for you: if you have ever seen a big pike chasing a small rainbow trout, you'll realize that it is very lucky to catch it; but there is one thing that any big pike can do, and that is swim faster than a baby pike.

Angling techniques, as we have seen, are a mixture of those deep rooted in time, and new, thoroughly modern developments mostly achieved from the 1950s onwards. Angling philosophies are much the same. Pike angling is today in a very healthy position. Whilst it is true that many of the debates one sees in the very lively modern presses are rehashes of old ideas, this is not necessarily a bad thing at all. We all have to go through the learning process (though I do wish more people would read!), and out of that process the germs of thoroughly new ideas come about. I'll end this section with one such: who would have considered that fishing a static plug on the bottom would catch pike? It's happened twice to me in my life, and I dismissed the events as total flukes – but I am probably wrong.

PIKE LITERATURE

As I have written this, I have already mentioned most of the great tomes (and see the table on page 68 for a list). Today there are many experienced pikers, and many books, mostly very good indeed, but between the old days (up to Craig, say) and the present time there have been some very important books, often dealing with quite different aspects of piking. Thus two of the most inspirational were Fred Buller's *Pike!* (1971) and ... *Mammoth Pike* (1979).

These were not about the kinds of piking covered in *Fishing for Big Pike*, but more about legendary big pike and the traditional approaches. They are, arguably, the two most important books on pike in modern times. Not perhaps in the same mould, and perhaps not with the same wide-ranging inspiration, but Clive Gammon's *Hook, Line and Spinner* certainly took up the Thurlow-Craig cudgels and added to them. Dennis Pye's exploits impressed many people, but only a small volume testifies to his skills: I think the press exploits had a bigger impact than *The Way I Fish* (1964). Then there was *Big Pike* (1965) by Geoffrey Bucknall: like most of his work, it was high quality, superb writing, and he probably did what Fred Buller didn't, namely put big pike angling in perspective, just before the technical and philosophical revolution took place. So although it became quickly out of date in one sense, it certainly marked a milestone in piking literature.

There is a whole group of modern books that improved on *Fishing for Big Pike*, and my favourites in this respect are John

INNOVATION IN PIKE ANGLING ~IN SUMMARY	pre-Berners	Berners	Walton	Nobbes	Pennel	Bickerdyke	Jardine	Senior	Martin	Spence	Spencer	Hill	Craig	MODERN PIKE ANGLING SCENE
Year of principle book	1496	1577	1682	1865	1888	1896	1900	1907	1928	1936	1944	1951		1950s---
herring deadbaits	?	→			? ?									to present
threaded trace		→												to present
static deadbaits	?	→												1950s to present
sunken float rig		→												1960s to present
attractor smells		→												1960s to present
wire traces, fixed leads														1950s to present
baked timber		→												to 1960s
dyed lines	?	→												1950s to present
ledgered baits	?	→												1950s to present
free-line rigs		→												1950s to present
eel deadbaits		anon 1957												1950s to present (especially 1980s)
spun deadbait			continued to 1950s											
legered livebaits	?													1950s to present
line clips														1980s to present
paternoster		?												
'walking baits'														
gorge fishing										ended in 1940s				1950s to present
trolling (≈ sink draw)														(in decline)
feeding patterns														1950s to present
'Bellars' hooks														1950s to present
half deadbaits														
artificials		?												
consecutive trace wires														1980s
growth rates														
Pennell tackle					to present									in decline
spinning flights					to present									in decline
spinning					to present									
outlawing of eye-socket hold														ended in 1900s finally
on-the-spot feeding														1950s to present
single strand wirekinks														
Gazette bung fishing														in decline today
sliding floats														
advanced paternoster rigs														widespread from 1970s
snap tackle with adjustable Ryder														
use of eels and smelt		?	?											widespread use in 1980s
use of artificials (spoons)														
'shoaling' of pike														hot spot theory
Jardine snaptackle						to present day								
butt ring line floatant dispenser														re-invented by E.T. in 1980s
fly fishing for pike								sporadic to present day						
Taylor wobbled deadbaiting								sporadic to present day						
Trent Otter spinning flight														rare in 1970s & 1980s
twitched deadbaits														
mackerel deadbaits														perfected in 1980s
drifter rigs														
use of American techniques														
modern conservation principles														

Watson's *A Piker's Progress* (1991); Mick Brown's *Pike Fishing: the Practice and the Passion* (1993); and Martin Gay's incorrectly titled *Beginners' Guide to Pike Fishing* (1975). There are, of course, many more informative and readable modern books on piking that I cannot deal with here – though I have them all! It is worth noting, finally, that there are far, far more books on piking now than ever there were in the historical past. That simply reflects the availability of the sport now, the advances, and the passion in which it is held.

THE PIKE ANGLERS' CLUB

This was founded in 1977 by myself (secretary) and Hugh Reynolds (treasurer) ex-the Pike Society, the secretary of which was Eric Hodgson. Eric worked on us, and we finally decided to give it a go. The Pike Society was short lived and a failure in that few people joined it. Because of our professional workload we had to run the club as a beneficial dictatorship. The first thing we did was choose our own president, namely Bill Chillingworth. The three of us ran the show for three years, and then handed over to John Watson, Martyn Page and Vic

Bellars in Norfolk – the new dictatorship, and so it went on, and goes on.

The PAC was very necessary, notably to fight the corner for pike angling and the pike ecosystem, but also to raise standards amongst pike anglers. This it did, and still does. The concept has spread, and today there are similar clubs in other European countries including Ireland, and there is a special club in Scotland, too. Any serious piker needs to join one of these bodies simply to put something into the sport and to enable the club officers to fight the good fight. Personally I learn so much from the club and its members, not to mention its magazine and its annual jamboree, that I can fully recommend it to anyone, inexperienced or not; the more members it has, the better will be your piking, and the safer the pike will be. The current president is Bill Winship, and all you need to do to join is write to Peter Green, 17 Lincoln Street, Wakefield, Yorkshire WF2 0BE. The Lure Anglers' Society can be joined by writing to Mike Lench, 21 Northumberland Avenue, Kidderminster, Worcs DY11 7AN; and the Pike Fly Fishers Association by writing to Peter Jones, 28 Crown Avenue, Holbeach St Marks, Spalding, Lincs PE12 8EU.

3. Big Pike on Artificials

by Mike Green

It was an eerie sensation, that December morning, gazing down at the misty grey surface of the River Nene at Lilford Bridge, knowing that some fifty-five years before, a small boy had looked down from the same spot, fascinated to see the roach and bleak darting around the surface, taking flies. In that moment a fisherman was born. I was that lad, and I can remember the occasion as if it were yesterday. There was an angler seated just below the bridge who, my father tells me, was Bert Tite of 'Tite and Garfirth' shoe company, a personal friend, and he was pulling out fish one after the other.

We set up our picnic twenty yards from Bert, and I, apparently, asked my parents if I could go and watch 'the fishing man'. An hour and a half later my father said to mother, 'Look, he's really interested in fishing; I shall have to get him a little rod.' 'Don't be silly, dear,' she replied, 'It would only be a five-minute wonder!'

Now, fifty-eight years later, I am as fanatical an angler as anyone I know! My knees went weak at the thought of that half century. The river was, no doubt, just the same, but I had changed quite a bit! Notwithstanding, I fished two miles of the Nene that morning, with a spinning rod and my favourite lure at the time, the Rebel J30, and landed sixteen pike up to 16lb – a great result! It is interesting that I have tried there many times since, and never done as well.

Once my enthusiasm was fired up I could never get enough fishing, and I remember many happy days pursuing chub, tench, bream, rudd, roach, perch and, of course, pike, with my father in and around Northamptonshire. One of my favourite adventures was catching minnows from the Ise Brook, carting them home in an old tin bait-can hooked over my handlebars, and waiting for Dad to come home from work. After tea he would take me up to Cransley reservoir (still a beautiful place to fish), and we would catch lovely bristling perch of 1 to 2½lb into the dusk. They just *loved* those poor little minnows !

In those far-off days most of the pike caught were killed and eaten. Filleted, skinned and soaked in salty water overnight, I remember them being really tasty, though of course I wouldn't dream of killing one nowadays (unless it was sick or injured).

When I was about seven years old Cliff Fieldhouse, a friend of my father, was to pick me up from home and take me to Sywell reservoir, livebaiting for pike. I recall there was a blizzard of snow, and, thinking my lift wasn't going to make it, howling inconsolably, to the consternation and disbelief of my mother! (He *did* eventually come, and we went – so all was well!)

When I was old enough to go on my own, my piking outfit consisted of a rod made from a tank aerial, and, as far as I

This beautiful pike caught on the River Nene in January 2006 weighed in at 28lb 8oz. At the time it was Mike's personal best for this river, and his best ever fish captured on fly.

remember it, an 'Intrepid' fixed-spool reel. The lure was either a rubber-headed 'Voblex' or a 'Veltic' bar-spoon. The largest pike I ever caught then weighed just 10lb (from Sywell), though on one occasion I was with my friend Tony Bean when a 'huge' (probably as much as 17lb) pike grabbed a Voblex at his feet and broke it – a sad moment, and I can see it as clearly now as I did then!

As an aside, it is interesting to remember that in those days no one, as far as I am aware, ever fished deadbaits!

May I say at this point that I felt both surprised and rather honoured when Bob asked me to write this chapter of the book. Despite what he might say, I do *not* regard myself as either 'expert' or 'authority' on any branch of angling, and am well aware that there are many pike fishermen out there whose catches of big fish would make my own seem meagre. Furthermore, as I wrote in a recent article in *Pikelines*, I sometimes feel rather a fraud being a member of the Northampton Specimen Group. Several of my fellow members are totally dedicated in targeting very large (and sometimes 'record') fish, no matter how long it takes. I, on the other hand, am just a lifelong compulsive fisherman who *has* to be out there doing it! I *love* catching big pike – but equally I enjoy catching plenty of modest specimens, in the knowledge that, sooner or later, a 'big one' will put in an appearance.

Having fun fishing is the 'name of the game' for me. Sitting behind a set of deadbait rods can bring great rewards (and sometimes a really big fish), and I do practise this style of piking when I feel a bit lazy; but I must admit that I can get (dare I say it?) rather bored when nothing is happening, and generally speaking, prefer the more mobile style of fly, lure or jerk fishing. This approach is also greatly favoured by Sam, my big black labrador, who is almost always with me. Travelling light, it is quite possible to cover several miles of river, and/or many different gravel pits during a day's fishing, and to put temptation in front of dozens (if not hundreds) of different fish. When conditions have been favourable and the fish obliging, my companion Tim Sumner and I have many times had thirty or more fish in a single day – and you never know when a real 'crocodile' may show up!

EARLY DAYS WITH THE FLY

My first experience of catching pike on fly was in the late 1960s when I became keen on trout fishing, encouraged by that expert nymph fisherman and top all-rounder Arthur Cove. Arthur took me to Grafham and started me off. I loved it right from the beginning, and was soon a season-ticket man, tying all my own flies, and so on. Rod Barley, another of Arthur's friends, became my regular trouting partner, and we have remained great friends ever since. At that time Grafham was *full* of pike, and I must confess that Rod and I looked on them as a bit of a nuisance! 'Bite-offs' were an every-trip experience, even on pheasant-tail

nymphs, necessitating retying the cast and droppers every time. Despite these feelings of annoyance, I can clearly remember the sadness I felt when a beautiful 25lb fish was killed by a trout fisherman after a long battle in Hill Farm bay. I can see it now, lying in the bottom of his boat, the large tandem baby-doll, intended for a big brownie, still firmly in its scissors. The angler was reluctant to get near enough to remove his fly even after the unfortunate fish had been clubbed to death. I thought what a shame it was, and what a thrill it must be to catch such a specimen on the fly by intention.

As a matter of interest, the pike were such a pest that protests were lodged with David Fleming-Jones, who was at that time in control of the fishing; and I was present when he said 'It's not a problem, because by the time a pike's big enough to eat a trout, it's too slow to catch one.' Can you believe it?! Soon after that Rod and I, just for devilment, arranged to meet an *Angling Times* photographer on the bank at Grafham on the last day of the season, and pretended to be pike fishing with what was thought of in those days as 'large' plugs. We never actually cast out, but the picture looked good in the paper and gave our fellow season-ticket holders a bit of a giggle. But the management didn't see the funny side of it, and we were promptly banned for fishing illegally! Such is life!

Strangely enough, the very next summer the pike and perch all contracted a strange disease, and many tons of dead fish were collected from Grafham's shores. At that stage I didn't think too much further about pike fishing, being more into trout, sea trout and salmon, and consequently my first big 'pike-on-fly' was caught 'by accident'. The story of its capture has an amusing side!

My best friend Ken Heath and I met many years ago shooting for geese in

Scotland, and in fact came within an atom of having a scrap! Fortunately (for me!) instead of exchanging blows, we started giggling, and have been close friends ever since. During this time I introduced Ken to fishing (mostly for salmon and trout), and I don't believe at the time he had had much contact with pike. On 23 December 1985 he had 'wangled' us a day's fishing on a private Cheshire Mere known as Maer Hall Lake, owned by one of his customers, and stocked with a few rainbows. We had the use of a tiny coracle of a boat, and the deal was that we were trout fishing. The owner, however, asked us to bring some spinning tackle as he had seen a big pike eating his rainbows, and we were requested to try to catch and remove it.

It was a lovely mild day, and we soon boated six or seven dark-coloured trout; then we had a 'spin' for an hour, as directed, but without success – not even a perch or a trout. I then decided to return to fly fishing and picked up my 9ft rod, loaded with floating line and size 8 black lure. On the very first cast I felt a great 'thump' and everything went solid, and I announced to Ken that something big had grabbed my fly. He was sure it was a snag, until the 'snag' suddenly ripped off twenty yards of line in five seconds, then stopped. 'Big pike,' I said; but why hadn't it bitten through the 6lb leader? Ten minutes later the mystery monster was towing the coracle round in slow circles at a depth of four or five feet.

I said, 'Ken, for Pete's sake, stand up and see if you can get a glimpse of this beast – if I lose it I must at least know what it was!'

He duly obliged, then blurted out, 'Oh, please no!' (or something like that!). I glanced up, and saw that he was clearly shaken.

'It's not a fish,' he whispered. 'Of course it's a fish,' I said, 'What else could it be?'

'It's a d.... great crocodile!' came the reply; and one look was enough to tell me that he really believed it! That told me all I needed to know, and I set about bringing the battle to a conclusion, whilst the white face at my side continued: 'Whatever that thing is, I do not want it in this boat with me!'

The rest of the story is fairly academic. I managed to lift the fish into the boat, and it weighed 25lb exactly, with the small lure firmly embedded in its scissors. We despatched the pike as we had been instructed – but it wasn't a complete waste, as she now stares defiantly down at me as I write, from the glass case on the wall.

That little adventure really boosted my enthusiasm for pike fishing, and I have been after them fairly regularly every winter since.

JERKING

I started reading about jerkbaits through the exploits of Derek Macdonald and Mick Brown, but at first wasn't overly influenced by them. I was catching plenty of pike on spinning tackle, using my favourite lures at the time – the likes of the Ondex, Rebel J 30, Shakespeare Big S – and didn't feel the need for anything different (one year I kept a tally, and recorded catching 303 pike, the biggest 23lb, and averaging about 6lb, almost all on lures). However, I saw the effectiveness of large artificials on Lake Nasser in Egypt, where I enjoyed four trips and caught some lovely Nile perch from the shore, including several sixty-pounders and a really massive specimen of 120lb. I tried these same lures – Bucher Depth Raiders, Rapala Shadraps – on pike, and with success, but felt they were not really any more effective than my normal and more lightweight lures.

Nevertheless I ordered a big jerkbait from Sue Harris, and fished it for fifteen

The reward for persistence – a 120lb Nile Perch caught from the shore of Lake Nasser on a Luhr-jenson fingerling after a sixty-minute battle.

minutes on a heavy spinning rod and 18lb *nylon* line – and I *hated* it: it was big, cumbersome and heavy, and I couldn't imagine any self-respecting pike going anywhere near it, never mind trying to eat it! Sue happily accepted it back into stock, but assured me that lots of big fish were being caught on such creations. I was not convinced – until one particular occasion totally changed my thinking.

The venue was Blithfield, a 900-acre trout water in Staffordshire, where my good friend George Meigh, a season-ticket holder, had invited me for a day's lure fishing for pike. He told me that 'Toby' spoons were the answer, but I chose to stick with my usual tactics. I liked the water immediately, and almost had a heart attack when a fish like a railway sleeper swirled at my lure five yards out! Later in the morning a chap came round a point and asked me if I had a camera. I confirmed that I had, and inquired if he had taken a big one. 'Not

bad,' he replied, quite calmly; and I thought, 'It'll be over twenty, anyway'. I accompanied the lucky angler, whom I now know as Rob Johnson, to his spot and made ready with the camera whilst he retrieved the sack. As he slid the fish out, my jaw dropped: I had never seen such a pike. It weighed 29lb 14oz, and it was immaculate !

After we watched it swim away, Rob showed me the Suick Thriller jerkbait it had taken. I also noted the short, stiff rod, the multiplier reel and strong braided line. At that point one of Rob's friends joined us; he had a similar outfit, and had himself caught a 20lb-plus pike that morning. That did it! I determined there and then that I *must* catch such a fish, whatever it took!

Step one was to invest in a genuine jerk rod, 50lb braided line and a Shimano Curado multiplier (a brilliant, reliable and trouble-free reel that I am still using today). Step two was to go 'cap in hand' to

Sue Harris again: this time I bought several 'Mean Thin Lizzies', and determined to give them a real try. From then my 'modus operandi' was to field two outfits: the new jerk tackle, and my old faithful lighter gear. Surprisingly, looking back, I still tended to favour the latter. One evening just before dusk I snagged up and broke off the J 30. I didn't bother to tie on another trace, but picked up the jerk rod – and at the first cast a 12lb pike engulfed the lure at my feet, and the next produced another smaller fish: this was impressive from a small lake where it was customary to catch a couple of small fish, but rarely a double. From this moment the heavier outfit became my first choice, and I noticed immediately that I started catching fourteens, sixteens and the occasional twenty from small dykes and pits that had previously only given up smaller specimens. Now I *was* convinced!

A REMARKABLE MORNING

I joined Blithfield as a full member with the sole idea of catching a 30lb pike. Just before the trout season opened, members and one guest were allowed two days pike fishing with lures, and I knew I just *had* to be there for that first day! Unfortunately I had only returned from a holiday in the Seychelles at 10pm the previous night; but after just three hours sleep and a fraught journey, regular piking partner Tim Sumner and I arrived well before first light.

There were already several cars at Watery Lane, a well known 'pikey spot, so we chose the opposite side of the road dam to start. I showed Tim my outfit, but he didn't really like it. Whilst he was threading up his spinning rod I thought I may as well have a throw right in front of the car, despite the fact that another angler had just left there. On my second cast the water

just 'opened up', and a huge pike engulfed the Thin Lizzie !

'I'm in!' I shouted to Tim, 'And it's a *really* big one!' 'Jammy ol' so-and-so,' he murmured from the rear of the Discovery, 'OK, I'll be down there in a moment.'

Shortly afterwards another angler pulled up (still in the dark!), and I heard him say to Tim, 'Your mate's got a big fish on, by the look of it.' Slightly reluctantly, Tim wandered the twenty yards or so to where I had the pike now in the margin.

'Where is it, then?' he inquired. 'It's right in front of you!' I gasped; at which point the fish rolled on to its side.

'B... Hell!' he said, 'However big is *that*?! 'It *must* be a thirty!', I replied shakily. 'Looks forty to me!' came the response. The scales said 31lb 12oz, my biggest-ever pike, and totally immaculate; and so I had achieved my ambition twenty minutes into the season, and felt an overwhelming joy!

Mike Reay, the fishery officer and head bailiff arrived soon after: 'You've got it already then, have you?' he said. 'How did *you* know? It's still dark!'

'Word travels fast here,' he laughed (he knew how desperate I had been to get a thirty, and had seen the camera flash from the far shore). 'I just *knew* it would be you,' he said with a big grin.

I would have been totally happy with that catch for the whole year, but there was more to come – much more! This was going to be *the* morning of my fishing life!

Two hours later Tim and I had worked our way along the north shore to the lodge, without further incident. Whilst Tim was tying on a new trace, I had a quick throw in his spot whilst waiting – and my first cast had a fish flash at the lure! 'Was it big?' asked Tim; to which I replied, 'No, maybe 6 or 7lb.' Another cast in the same spot – and another big pike crashed into the jerkbait. My excitement was tempered by a slight twinge of guilt as I lifted out a second leviathan, as Tim clipped on a new spinner. This one went 28lb 10oz – almost too good to be true!

We then wandered back to the car and a welcome cup of tea, before driving round to the sailing club for a crack at the south shore. By this time there were quite a few anglers about, though no one seemed to be getting much. Tim had a 'follow and swirl' in one shallow bay, but that was it for another couple of hours and another two miles of bank. The lack of sleep was beginning to tell, despite all the excitement, so we agreed to call it a day at about 1pm. Ambling back in the direction of the vehicle, that same bay looked inviting, so we tried a few more casts. By this time we were both fishing jerkbaits, though Tim's was, of course, on his spinning gear – *not* the same, as I will explain later!

Nevertheless, I was so pleased when he hooked a pike – and before he landed it, I had one on, too! They weighed 13lb and 18lb, and we were well pleased. Just about exhausted, I announced to Tim that I would have just one more throw and that would be it. Astonishingly, after two 'jerks' there was a mighty eruption and I had hooked yet another big fish! It seemed beyond belief, but as I slid it on to the shoreline reeds we both knew it was another thirty! The scales said 31lb exactly: we were speechless!

The sequel to this story is that firstly, despite two years of trying with lures and flies, I never managed to catch another twenty from Blithfield (though I did get an eighteen on fly). Secondly, Tim jerked out a 31lb 8oz beauty twelve months later at the same venue; and I have never seen him with a spinning rod in his hand since!

Thirdly, if it all sounds a bit easy, Mike Reay told me later that fifty anglers caught just eleven pike that day, of which we'd had five – which only goes to show what a lucky star can do at times!

My lucky star has been looking after me fairly well during the last three or four pike seasons. I am always pleased to catch one 20lb fish over the winter, and I have managed at least one for the past decade or so, but lately my average has shot up. Last year I was fortunate enough to catch eight different twenties, with the largest at 29¾lb; of these, three were on fish baits, two on fly and three on jerkbaits. The previous season I had nine, though there were a couple of recaptures involved, but nevertheless things have gone well. Having said that, I have been retired for three and a half years now and, consequently am able to fish more or less any time, and take advantage of favourable conditions. A good example of my 'jam-spangle' (as we say in these parts!), took place one December evening, last year.

Bob, 'Spike' Harrison and I had enjoyed a successful day on a gravel pit complex, and, as the light started to fade, we found ourselves in a very likely looking bay. The water was seven or eight foot deep, and gin clear with a carpet of Canadian pondweed; it screamed pike, and I felt it *must* produce! Sure enough, on my very first cast a nice fish slammed into my silver jerkbait. I told Bob I was into a decent one, and he made his way along to me as I lifted it out, after a spirited battle. The pike was in perfect order, but looked as if it would not quite reach the 'magic' twenty mark. However, we both thought it was worth weighing and photographing. I laid the fish carefully on some dampened reeds and covered it up with more of the same, whilst the other two went off to retrieve camera and scales from the boat we had been using on an adjacent lake.

They seemed to be gone for an age, but the pike was lying quietly and, having nothing better to do, I thought I may as well have another cast. You've guessed it already … as the bait hit the water there

The 31lb 12oz pike that started my magic morning at Blithfield.

The 28lb 10oz pike that followed.

The 31lb pike that completed an incredible morning!

Pike of 18lb 12oz and 23lb 12oz taken in two casts at dusk on a gravel pit.

was a mighty swirl and my arm was nearly wrenched out of its socket as another big fish crashed into the lure! I could hardly believe it! This one went crazy, and I felt sure it was bigger than the first. At the same time I noticed that it was only lightly hooked, and became extremely anxious: if I were to lose it they would surely never believe me! As I eased its great head over the edge of the reeds, sure enough the silver jerk flew out; but in a flash I had my hand inside the gill cover and slid my prize to safety.

I stared down, smiling with joy! This one was definitely over twenty, and like the first fish, was fin and scale perfect! I laid her

gently next to her 'sister' and covered them up, just in time to see the other two making their way back. Preparations were soon made for the weighing and photos.

'Right then, which one do you want first, the small one or the big one?' I beamed! 'You've never had another one, have you?' said Bob in some disbelief. I grinned and lifted the reeds, revealing the lovely brace of pike – taken in two casts! They weighed 18lb 12oz and 23lb 12oz, and I went home that night a very happy fisherman.

Another 'red letter' occasion is worthy of mention. In Northamptonshire we are blessed with a wealth of gravel pits all along the Nene and Ouse river valleys. I wouldn't like to guess just how many lakes there are in the Midlands, and a great many of them are hardly ever fished. Furthermore it is not always clear who owns them, but the situation is such that, within reason, you can more or less 'wander at will' ('guesting', I believe it is called).

Unusually the river had not 'produced the goods' that particular Saturday morning, so I decided to do a bit of exploring. The lakes in question looked very 'pikey', but a couple of hours' walking and jerk casting proved fairly fruitless. Eventually I found a water that looked so perfect it just *had* to perform, and sure enough, a dozen casts notched up four fish, with the best about 8lb. This was more like it! I phoned Tim with the report, and plans were made for a dawn foray the next morning. And so it was: we set up with two livebait rods each, and jerk rods, just in case.

All was quiet for a couple of hours, so we moved away from each other a little, and recast. I had two roach as baits, one paternostered and the second on a sailfloat, which made its way slowly out eighty or ninety yards, but with no 'customers'. Being somewhat impatient by nature, I wound in my bait rods and wandered off to the right, where there seemed to be some likely-looking bays, with my jerk rod. Almost immediately I had a good take and caught a seven-pounder, which was quickly followed by a second, this one just making double figures.

'Jerks rule OK,' I said to myself as I made my way to the next point. A long cast from this spot, two jerks – and there was pandemonium! There was a swirl that looked as though it could have been made by a hippopotamus, and everything went solid. The slow, heavy nods of the pike's head told me straightaway that without a doubt this was a *beast*! I struggled to slacken off the drag as the big fish decided it didn't like this game and would be better off on the far side of the lake! My heart was beating excitedly as, yard by yard, the fish gave in to the pressure and eventually made a close pass in the gin-clear water.

'Oh *please* don't let this one come off,' I blurted out aloud, 'I really *need* this fish!' And my fears were confirmed because as I got it to the reed margin, the bait flew out of its great jaws, and it just lay there looking at me! Without a second's hesitation I threw myself in its direction, and managed to 'wrestle' the monster on to the soft reedbed, getting half soaked in the process! But it was well worth it as I looked down at what was surely a gravel-pit thirty-pounder. I just couldn't believe my good fortune! With shaking hands I retrieved a rather damp mobile phone out of my pocket and phoned Tim.

'What's happening?'

'Get yourself round here Tim, I've just had a thirty!' There was a short silence, followed by: 'You're joking!'

'No really, it's lying here in front of me,' I assured him.

'On a livebait?'

'No, on that new jerkbait I've just made.' Another pause, then: 'I'm on my way!' I always carry some soft rope as an emergency 'stringer', so I tied the monster to a tree and left it lying quietly in the marginal reeds while I went for the weighsling, scales and camera. On the way I met Tim coming the other way, and pointed out where I'd left the fish. 'You can't miss it,' I said.

When I returned with the necessary Tim was smiling. 'Well done, Master,' he said. 'That is the biggest pike I have ever seen in my life!' (remember he was with me when I caught the Blithfield thirties).

We took some pictures and then set up the scales. It may sound a little ungrateful to relate that we were both surprised and a little disappointed when the dial showed 28lb 8oz!

'They must be wrong,' exclaimed Tim; but his scales showed exactly the same weight, so that was that! Nevertheless I was absolutely delighted with such a wonderful fish; we watched it swim gracefully away, none the worse for the experience. I subsequently sent a picture to Steve Ormrod at the PAC, who sent his congratulations and advised me to check my scales. I did, and they were spot on!

Both Tim and I have noticed that it is often on a bad day, when nothing much seems to be happening, that the big fish will show up. This has occurred enough times to be more than coincidence, and is excellent inspiration to 'keep going' no matter how hopeless the prospects may seem to be. I well recall one particular morning on the River Nene when it was so icy cold in the melting frost and fresh east wind that I just couldn't throw out my fly any more. I gave up, and watched Tim persevering with his jerk rod, while I endeavoured to get some life back into my frozen limbs. Though we hadn't had a pull or any sign of a fish between us till then, at the next weir the jerkbait was stopped with a solid thump, and Tim landed a terrific-

A magnificent pike of 28lb 8oz from a local gravel pit on a home-made jerkbait.

looking pike of 21lb 8oz! This was a marvellous fish for the river, and a well deserved reward for 'keeping at it'!

On another occasion, again on the Nene but on a different stretch, we had 'leap-frogged' at least a mile of the river with our jerk rods, but without a result of any kind. This was unusual, as the water was 'greeny' clear and in good order. However, the sun was shining down from a clear blue sky, which was not ideal, and nor was the fact that it was again really cold following a

clear night and very sharp frost. I was starting to lose confidence.

'We've had it, Tim,' I said, 'It's just too freezing cold – they're not going to have it!'

'We'll get them,' replied Tim optimistically, 'There'll be a "nest" of takers somewhere, and don't forget this is the sort of day you come across a *really* big one!' We stopped in the shelter of a small spinney for a welcome cup of coffee and a warm-up, and as soon as we started again, Tim announced that he'd had a pull. Next cast

RIGHT: Tim's 21lb 8oz pristine fish from the Nene in 'brass monkey' weather!

BELOW: Never caught before? A wonderful fish on a 'hopeless' morning!

he caught a modest (but welcome) fish. And then, before he'd even unhooked it, I saw a big silver flash and my bait came to an abrupt halt. It felt as though I had snagged a tree root, but not for long, as this fish realized its mistake and went into a pattern of heavy plunges and violent head shaking. I was a bit anxious about this behaviour, but in fact needn't have worried, as the rear hooks were securely lodged in the scissors.

Tim very confidently lifted out my prize and announced that it must weigh between 23 and 24lb. I agreed, but the scales said 22lb exactly. But what a beauty, and on a 'hard' day! Tim had been right (as he often seems to be!), and we were both delighted. In fact we fished on, and caught a few more, though of course no more 'crocs'! The moral? Never give up!

JERKBAITING: TACKLE AND TECHNIQUES

I think it is fairly well recognized and acknowledged that the ideal rod for this style of lure fishing should be about 6 to 7ft in length, and quite stiff in action. It really must be stiff, because a rod with too soft an action would not be able to impart the sudden, darting acceleration so essential to the success of this method. I have seen anglers using fixed-spool reels in conjunction with jerks, but would not care to do so myself. The weight of the lure and the rather vigorous rod action required puts quite a strain on the tackle, and without a doubt the modern, easy-to-use multipliers are far more suitable.

As to line, I would go so far as to say that it *has* to be braid. No one would be daft enough to suggest that you couldn't catch a fish using monofil, but for the same reason that you need a stiff-action short rod, with stretchy nylon it is more or less impossible to get that essential 'snap' into the movement of the bait. I would advise a minimum of 50lb bs, which may seem excessive, but as I said above there is inevitably a lot of heavy strain on the equipment, and I personally tend to use 80lb bs. Even this is reasonably thin, enabling casts of fifty yards and more to be made effortlessly – and anyway, who wants to break on a fish?

At the business end, a stiff wire trace of 12 to 15in is absolutely essential in order to prevent the bait tangling up. A good jerkbait, worked in the correct manner, will sweep from side to side at 90 degrees to the direction of the angler, and in fact, given enough 'slack' between jerks, can easily end up pointing *away*! A soft wire trace in this situation would be completely inappropriate, and would become entangled with the large treble hooks on almost every cast. Even using a stiff trace, this happens occasionally anyway and just has to be endured...

Jerk traces are widely available (including some rather attractive 'titanium' ones), but Tim and I prefer to make our own from 1mm welding wire, and these have proved to be very successful; no matter how many times we have to re-straighten them, I don't remember one ever breaking. We experimented quite extensively in the early days, and have come to the definite conclusion that a strong link-swivel is ideal at the lure end, but there should be *no* swivel at the line end, as again, this tends to tangle.

Regarding the lures themselves, the magazines are full of mouth-watering selections for your perusal, and I've little doubt that most, if not all, would catch fish in suitable conditions and situations. I like to make my own from hardwoods such as mahogany and teak, and although it's a rather time-consuming task, it's enjoyable, and I find it very rewarding catching pike on my own creations.

Making Your Own Jerkbaits

For those fishermen who fancy making their own baits, perhaps I might offer a few basic guidelines:

(1) Cut out the shape and size required. I advise somewhere between 5 and 8in (13–20cm) in length, and either round or 'slab-sided' in profile, according to choice. The round-sectioned type tend to be 'gliders', traversing from side to side in long sweeping glides, whereas the 'flat' ones can glide or 'flip' this way and that, depending on the pattern. Making the 'round' ones ideally necessitates some sort of lathe, and I bought a basic bandsaw to speed up my production of the other sort.

(2) Round off the edges with a sharp knife, then file and sandpaper to a smooth finish. (I have a Dremmel Sander, which again makes life slightly easier.)

(3) Make location holes for the hook-hangers with a 1ml drill, stopping about ¼in short of the length of the hanger (if you neglect this precaution you will surely break some of the hook-hangers trying to screw them in, which is annoying, to say the least!).

(4) Insert the hook-hangers (with Araldite, if you like, though I never bother and have not had one pull out on me yet!).

(5) With a ⅜in (9mm) wood drill, create holes for the lead-weighting (as shown in the diagram – approximately ½ to ¾in (13 to 19mm) deep).

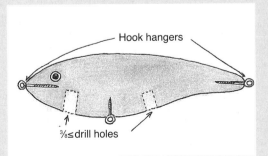

Hook hangers

⅜≤ drill holes

(6) Heat lead to its molten state in an aluminium basin, and carefully pour it into the holes until they are almost full to the top (maybe ⅛in (3mm) short of the surface of the lure?).

(7) Paint the bait with white enamel (or anything you like, really); when it's dry it is then ready for 'trimming'.

(8) *This is most important:* Fix split rings and treble hooks to the lure, and then place it in a container of water to see how it behaves. Adjust the action/sink rate by either drilling out some lead, or adding some if required. Ideally the bait should sink with a steady horizontal motion, not too head first, and certainly not tail first. The sink rate you can decide for yourselves, but I find the very best gliding actions come with quite slow-sinking baits (about 1ft (30cm) every 3sec).

(9) When you are completely satisfied with the last stage, it is time to dry off the bait and then fill the holes with plastic wood/fast Araldite.

(10) Smooth off the Araldite to a flush finish with a file/sandpaper, and you are now ready to complete the job. Give the lure two or three coats of white enamel, followed by the colours/ pattern of your choice. For the finishing touch, two or three coats of exterior varnish or two-part epoxy are advised. This ensures a nice, glassy, waterproof appearance, and helps to protect the bait from the pike's razor-like teeth (though they still rip it to bits eventually!)

(11) Eyes are again a matter of choice; I tend to favour epoxy-moulded eyes, but I think they're mainly for me. In fact, whether the lure has painted, stuck-on holographic ones or no eyes at all, it probably doesn't make much difference to the pike when they're in the mood, and when I fished with Charlie Bettell down in Norfolk, I noticed that, other than varnish, he doesn't paint his lures at all! It's the *action* of the bait that's all-important.

Whatever your baits look like, it is the jerking technique that is all-important. There's nothing to it – although having said that, every single person I have introduced to the method (including even Bob, at first) has made the same basic mistake, namely too much winding and not enough jerking! The secret of the jerk's success is the sudden acceleration and dramatic change of direction. This is achieved by a short, sharp 'tap' of the rod tip (up, down or sideways, it doesn't matter), followed by a pause and slackening off to allow the bait to glide away laterally. When executed correctly, pike cannot resist it (apart from those days when they won't look at anything). Furthermore, as I may have mentioned earlier, jerkbaits will definitely tempt big fish as well as small ones. If you haven't yet tried the method, give it a go: you will be amazed at the results !

Having said that, and although I have enjoyed tremendous success with jerkbaits, you may find it rather strange that, these days, it is not, in fact, my method of first choice. There are two reasons for this: first, with very strong, non-stretch line and a rod like a poker, unless the pike is a double or larger, you don't really tend to get much of a fight after the first arm-wrenching pull. Using light spinning gear, by comparison, at least you can enjoy a bit of a battle.

Allied to the above – and this to me is more important – small pike tend to be 'skull-dragged' in, confused and with barely a waggle, and then they go totally demented at your feet, with 2/0 and 3/0 trebles flying in all directions. Occasionally they can become foul-hooked by the flailing treble, and I regret to say that in one or two instances I have had to remove such a hook from a fish's eye. I have found this most upsetting, rare as it may have been, and that is why, whenever it is feasible, I prefer to try for them by fly fishing.

Incidentally, whilst on the subject, during hand-landing and unhooking fish, those flying hooks are just as likely to catch you, so extreme caution is advised. Once when fishing alone in a deluge of rain, I had the rather harrowing experience of a 9lb pike on the front treble and my middle finger on the other! I recall ripping out the 2/0 hook on the *third* attempt, not an event I would care to repeat in a hurry! Then, having stemmed the flow of blood, and because the pike were 'on the go', I decided to carry on in the downpour, and in the next bay, hooked and landed a twenty-three-pounder! I don't have to tell you that I was considerably more careful unhooking that one! A protective glove is invaluable in preventing accidents, even though it slightly hampers your efforts to gill out a fish, and barbless hooks are also a good idea, for obvious reasons.

FLY FISHING: TACKLE AND TECHNIQUES

Whenever possible I would fly fish in preference to any other method. Sometimes it can be more awkward and frustrating, but when success comes the rewards are beyond comparison. To witness that big crocodile-like head and gaping jaws engulf your fly is a truly heart-stopping experience, and I would encourage all keen pike anglers to give it a try. The tackle you need is simple, lightweight and not necessarily too expensive.

Rods

To cast a 6in to 8in (15–20cm) fly safely the outfit must be fairly powerful. I use the 'Champion Piker' 9ft rod marketed by Bob Church, which, I have to say, has revolutionized the whole procedure. In the early days I experimented with all sorts of rods, mostly 8- and 9-weight; I even 'made' my own from a cut-down Bruce and Walker 15ft salmon rod, and indeed enjoyed considerable success, including a 'fat' 25lb 8oz beauty from an estate lake (and which was still my PB fly-caught pike until January 2006). Apart from the 'home-made' one, which was ill-balanced and a bit heavy, all the others were just too light and inadequate to push out that big fly, especially into any sort of breeze. At times it was positively dangerous, and more than once I ended up with the fly stuck in my coat or hat.

When Bob brought out the 'Champion Piker' 12-weight rod, with shooting-head lines to match, I immediately fell in love with its steely action combined with its light weight. I was astonished when my very first tentative cast sailed out an effortless thirty yards, and furthermore quickly realized that, within reason, wind direction became much less important: a real step forwards! I now also use a 9ft, 12-weight, Shimano fly rod that again is excellent. Both of these rods are powerful enough to handle a big pike, yet flexible enough to enjoy a good scrap from a five-pounder.

Lines, Traces and Reels

As indicated above, I advise an 11- or 12-weight shooting head, or weight-forward line; these come in different sinking rates, from floater to very fast sinker, enabling you to fish depths of two to thirty-plus feet (60cm to 9m). If you wanted to make a start with just one line, I would probably suggest an intermediate/very slow sinker, as this seems to be the most versatile. In shallow water you can retrieve fast, and in deeper lakes/rivers, 'count it down' before commencing the retrieve. Personally I have four different lines: floater, intermediate, medium sinker and very fast sinker, and use them all at various times. The last mentioned is most useful on big lakes and

reservoirs, where the depth may be thirty feet (9m) or more. It can also be employed in any depth of water using a short leader combined with a buoyant fly, 'booby style' – but more of that later.

Speaking of the leader, I generally use about six feet (2m) of 25lb bs Amnesia clear nylon. Longer might give slightly better presentation (though the pike don't seem to mind!), but remember that the longer the leader, the more difficult (and dangerous?) it is to cast. Of course, a 12 to 15in (30–38cm) wire trace is required at the 'business' end to prevent 'bite-offs'. As ever, these are commercially available, but, being a DIY type, I prefer to rely on my own. I like 20lb QED traditional wire, but there are many alternatives. At the leader end I use a small, oval, stainless-steel ring (as used in carp fishing), and at the other a stainless clip to which the 'fly' is attached. Recently I have been experimenting with 120lb bs nylon as an alternative to wire. Obviously it is much thicker and more clumsy-looking, but it is transparent, not prone to kinking, and thus far I have not had a 'toothy monster' come anywhere close to biting through it. The jury is still out on this one, however, but you may care to give it a try.

There are numerous 'wide-arbour' fly reels available these days, which help to prevent 'memory coils' in the line/backing, and, in my opinion, almost any one will do. Strong as they are, pike don't tend to go screaming off like bonefish (that frequently go 150 yards in one rush!), so any reel that will hold the line and 75 to 100 yards of backing should be more than adequate.

Flies

So we have rod, reel, line and backing, leader and trace, and now we come to the fly itself. The term 'fly' is perhaps a misnomer for a 6–8in (15–20cm) tinsel and fibre lure, which after all isn't meant to represent a fly at all, but rather a fish, mouse, frog, or in fact any type of living thing suitable for a pike to devour! Nevertheless, since the method involves a fly-casting action, we shall continue to refer to our creations as 'flies'. They are now widely available to buy in a wide variety of shapes and colours, mostly tied on 3/0 to 6/0 lightweight Aberdeen-type sea hooks. I honestly do not believe that the pattern or colour matters a great deal when the pike are 'up for it', but, having said that, we all feel we *must* have an assortment to look at in the box – and you never know, it just *might* make a difference on the day!

I enjoy making my own, with crystal hair, sparkle-chenille, lureflash and the new 'wonder material' slinky fibre: the latter is extremely hydrophobic (meaning that it doesn't absorb water and therefore remains light in weight and easy to cast), and it also has a lovely fluent action sub-surface, as well as being very robust and tooth-resistant. I highly recommend this material to all prospective pike fly tiers! I tie my flies mainly in pearly white, yellow, hot orange and black, and they have all worked extremely well on their day. I nearly always add eyes and epoxy-type heads, but in truth it's probably more for myself than for the fish! Bob and I shared a nice catch of seven doubles to 19lb at Chew Valley Lake, all taken on pearly blue and white flies with no eyes and no heads – so you can draw your own conclusions. I shall continue to 'tart them up', however, as they certainly look better to me – and confidence, as you well know, is a great thing!

My early efforts consisted of 6in- (15cm-) long fibres tied in at the head of the hook. These worked beautifully in the water when they weren't tangled around the hook shaft, but unfortunately this happened on one out of every three casts! The thought of a tangled, and therefore ineffec-tive, fly being presented to, and 'spooking' a possible thirty-pounder, was more than I could bear. I then tried 'Matuka'-type patterns with bunches of fibres tied in just along the back of the hook, and these caught fish and didn't tangle, but to my mind they didn't look as good. This problem was solved by my good friend Stewart Whybrow, who tied his fibres in criss-cross fashion, doing a 'figure-of-eight' with the tying silk. This resulted in a mass of fibres spreading out from the hook in all directions, it eliminated tangling, and the fly looked good in the water. If the end result appeared too bulky it could be 'attacked' with hairdresser's thinning scissors to produce the desired effect.

The body and head of the fly I normally tie using sparkle-chenille, and having built up the head to the required shape and size, I tease on some five-minute Araldite to the fibres. As it starts to harden it is a simple matter to mould the head gently to the required shape. The eyes can then be added, and I usually seal them in position with a second small application of the glue. It's easy, and much fun can be had designing and making your own patterns.

I have found that when the pike are in the mood, they will attack the fly as readily as any other lure. Given that a jerkbait can be readily cast fifty or sixty yards, and the fly, shall we say, half of that distance, you would expect the jerk method to produce more fish – and in truth it generally does! Tim and I have often had friendly competitions, however, and the first time we did it at one stage the score was eight fish each! (The jerk eventually came out winner at twelve versus nine, but with no disgrace to the fly!) The indisputable facts are that:

- it is much more fun with the fly;
- the fight is ten times better; and
- the take can be breathtaking when the fly is in sight.

RIGHT: A 7in fly doesn't look so big in the jaws of a 20lb pike!

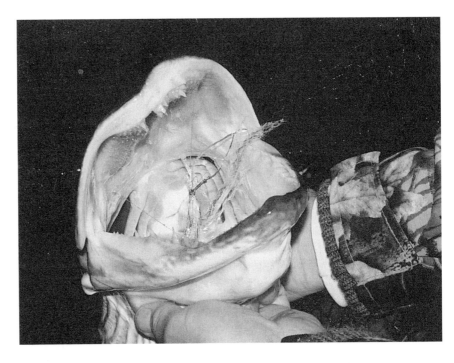

BELOW: A Fenland gravel pit 21lb 6oz on fly. Joy at the end of a hard day!

The most unforgettable and impressive take I have ever experienced to date took place on a Fen gravel pit where I was sharing a boat with Bob. We each had a livebait out on roving float tackle, and in addition Bob was having a few throws with the jerk rod, whilst I flogged away with a 7in pearly white fly on a slow-sink fly line. The water depth was 11ft (3.3m), and the water itself absolutely gin clear. It had been fairly quiet, but we kept moving position every so often, and I kept throwing my fly out in all directions, more because I *love* doing it, rather than with any great expectation of success. Then towards dusk, and without any warning, as my fly came into view for the thousandth time, a huge head appeared behind it and the fly disappeared into the cavernous jaws!

I hit it hard twice (of which more later), and I swear the pike looked confused. It then became angry as it flared its gills and tried to shake out the hook, which fortunately was well back in its mouth and secure. It seemed to us both that the pike's head doubled in size as it performed this tactic, and I don't think either of us will ever forget that dramatic sight! The fish then turned and shot off like a bullet, testing my tackle to the limit for several minutes before Bob was able to net this game specimen; it weighed 21lb 6oz. The satisfaction of catching such a fish on a self-tied fly, and after persevering all day, is, I can assure you, immeasurable!

Other necessary items advised for pike fly fishing are unhooking pliers, and a decent pair of polarized protective glasses. Being hit in the face (or worse, in the eye), by a 6/0 hook doing 80mph (130km/h) would be catastrophic, but this is an ever-present possibility, particularly in windy conditions: so be careful, and cast within your limits. Finally, if you are fishing from the bank side, some form of line tray is also an essential to prevent your line becoming caught up in thistles or other vegetation. (From a boat this is not so important, though I still tend to use one, especially in windy conditions.) Commercial line trays are readily available, but I use a modified washing-up bowl, as recommended by Alan Hanna in his excellent video *Fly Fishing for Big Pike*. Speaking of videos, there is another one featuring Larry Dalberg called *Fly Fishing for Pike*, and I defy any piker to watch the exhilarating action in this one without an increased heart rate!

My best results have invariably been in clear water, or when it is basically clear with a slight tinge of green. Muddy water or thick algal suspensions are absolutely hopeless, in my experience. The River Nene in my area can be brilliant during the winter when it is clear or 'greeny clear' after a flood, but if it has any colour you would not think it contained pike at all! Ask the match fishermen: they love a bit of colour as it means 'bite-offs' are rare, whereas in clear conditions the pike often

drive them to despair. One of my local lakes, which in the past had been good for fish up to 11 or 12lb, was full of green algae for several months, and correspondingly hopeless. Then on one of my general fly-fishing 'walkabouts' I was delighted to see that it had cleared nicely, and in two hours I banked *eight* pike, including one at 13¾lb, and my first twenty of the season at 20lb 4oz – quite a result, and great fun! So never write off any lake, no matter how small, as being unlikely to hold any big pike, as there may always be one there somewhere!

Since writing this I have had another nice pike from the same lake at 23lb, this time on a jerkbait – a different fish and proof that you never *do* know what is in there!

OTHER LURES

As you may have gathered, by this stage I spend most of my pike-fishing time fly fishing, if it's feasible, or alternatively casting jerkbaits. But we must not forget that there are legions of other different lures available, and I am sure some of these may represent many anglers' first-choice favourites.

Sometimes if I am fun-fishing small dykes, ponds or streams, where the majority of pike are likely to be small, and the vegetation/tree cover precludes the possibility of fishing the fly, I enjoy turning back the clock and trying for them with a light spinning outfit. This was my standard technique in pre-jerk days, and now, as then, can be hugely successful. My personal favourite lures for this approach are:

- The Rebel J 30 jointed crankbait
- The Ondex bar spoon (gold and silver)
- The Storm-Jointed Thunderstick
- The Shakespeare Big S diving crankbait

My son James with a nice pike of 19lb 8oz caught on light spinning tackle and a Rebel J 30. I took the same fish two years later at 25lb 8oz on fly, my best pike on a fly rod until a 28lb 8oz pike in January 2006.

Of course there are countless alternatives, and many of you will have your own 'specials', but I have caught many hundreds of pike on the above selection. Small lures tend, on the whole, to catch smaller pike, but there are always exceptions. I have caught several 20lb fish on Ondexes and J 30s, and a friend of mine once had a fabulous, immaculate twenty-five-pounder first cast with *my* spinning rod and Big S after arriving mid-morning just for a chat! Unusually I hadn't had a single offer that morning, with two sail-floated roach working really hard. And just to rub salt into the wound, this friend, having had his triumphant photo taken with the fish, went off shopping with his wife, while I fished on – and *blanked*! Life can be harsh sometimes!

With regard to the Ondex, as it comes it has one big drawback, which is that it is very light weight and therefore won't cast very well. I always wrap the body with lead wire or foil, coat it with Araldite, and then paint it red or silver; it then casts far better, and the action doesn't seem to be affected.

Also, whilst speaking of the Ondex, even though it is without doubt a highly successful and inexpensive lure, I have always felt that even the largest one (size 6) is rather small. With this in mind I obtained some 70mm blades and other components from my friend Nick Green at DIY Lures and Flies, and reproduced an Ondex 'Look-alike' but with a lead body, and about three times the size of the original. The 'G.O.', or Giant Ondex as my friends and I call it, has also been a great fish catcher!

If you are nostalgic, don't forget that old traditional lures such as the Colorado and kidney spoons still work today as they did in yesteryear. I'm not keen on either personally, but recently Bob himself showed me how successful they can be, with a fine catch of pike to 13lb from one of our favourite gravel pits.

One traditional and consistently effective lure that I *do* like is the standard large (6in/15cm) copper spoon, and I have seen many quality fish taken on these in the last two or three seasons. They often seem to work well on trout-reservoir pike, and should really find a place in everyone's lure bag.

Other lures that I *know* are extremely successful but which I don't really like are spinnerbaits, and heavy rubber lures such as the Bulldawg. I can't explain my lack of enthusiasm for these; maybe it's because most of my piking takes place on waters with a maximum depth of 12ft (3.6m) or so, and many at half of that. If I were to spend much time on trout reservoirs or deep glacial lakes such as Windermere, I'm sure I would soon develop more of a liking for them; as it is, I feel I am not qualified to comment on them. The times I have tried with them, it has been with little confidence, and so equally little success; but were I to drag a thirty-five-pounder off the bottom in 35ft of water on a 'Dawg', no doubt I would quickly show it more loyalty. As ever, we tend to use our favourites for most of the time we spend fishing, and so they tend to remain our 'hot lures'. A lure you don't really like doesn't tend to be much used, and so is unlikely to gain in popularity.

Surface Lures

My experience with churning, spluttering surface working lures is also rather limited, although unlike the 'Dawgs' and spinnerbaits, I *do* like the idea of them, both in fly and lure form. Some of my friends, including Bob, have caught some really nice fish from the surface, with some enviably dramatic strikes. My pike fishing tends to be mainly an autumn/winter activity, because in warmer conditions I worry about the ability of the fish to recover. For instance, fishing with Bob last year in the late summer on one of our favourite gravel pits, it was quite warm, and we decided to have a half an hour on the jerks.

Almost immediately I hooked a lean, but very fit pike of about 18lb, which fought well. I hand held it in the water for a few seconds whilst removing the hooks, but then had to steady it for some three or four minutes until it recovered and sailed slowly off back to the depths. Then three days later a friend found a fish of the same size belly up in the same area, surely the same one! This upset me considerably, as that specimen would have been a good twenty in the winter months, and it all seemed rather a needless waste.

Similarly I have had zander give up on me in July/August, despite the most gentle and careful handling, which is also a great shame (though they are never wasted, as my wife, Sally, thinks they eat better than plaice!).

Nevertheless I intend to put in a bit more effort into surface flies and lures in future, as the picture of that frantic smash-take is so appealing. Another of my forward plans is to experiment with them in the dark on those mild autumn evenings, as I anticipate that it could be most exciting and rewarding. I recall a clear, shallow Staffordshire lake, well frequented by anglers, dog walkers and picnickers, especially in good weather. Daytime piking proved relatively unproductive, but after dark the bigger fish lost some of their caution, and some nice specimens were landed on jerkbaits and wobbled deadbaits.

Crankbaits

I believe the current British record pike of about 46lb was taken on a Creek Chub Pikie crankbait from Llandegfedd a few seasons ago, so obviously this type of lure is not to be ignored. For the few who don't know, they are basically fish, frog or mouse-shaped baits with a diving vane at the front, which causes the lure to dive and 'wiggle' when 'cranked' or etrieved. The reel can be a multiplier or fixed spool, depending on the size and weight of the lure.

The retrieve can be a straight wind, or erratic, with pauses and spurts. Jerking the rod will also impart extra movement and attractiveness, and once again I strongly advise braided line as opposed to nylon, as it is thinner for the same strength and, perhaps more importantly, has virtually no stretch. The basic rule regarding the diving vane is that the narrower the angle to the line direction, the deeper the dive and the tighter the 'wiggle'. Conversely, the greater the angle, the shallower the dive and the wider and more dramatic the 'wiggle'. Some lures, like the ABU 'Hi-Lo', sport a hinged and adjustable vane, allowing variations in the working depth/action. Crankbaits can be floaters, slow or fast sinking, and you can also have a floater that will dive deep when cranked hard, for example the 'Big Mac' and the Luhr-Jensen 'Fingerling', which tempted my PB shore-caught Nile perch at 120lb.

Floating baits are useful in weedy situations, where you can stop winding and allow the lure to surface (or nearly so) over a shallow bar or weedbed, before cranking it down again into deeper water.

Jigbaits

'Jigging' is another method of which I have little experience; however, this is due to change in the near future, as I have every intention of trying for zander with jig tackle this coming season. The lure itself is invariably fashioned with a weighted head and the hook 'point up', which helps to make it snag free (though not always). Having cast to the desired spot, the jig bait is allowed to sink to the bottom or required depth, then fished back in a series of jerks. This creates a sort of 'sink-and-draw' motion, which can be very effective at waking up fish that are lying on the river/lake bed, and are reluctant to move far to chase a bait fishing in mid-water. The 'point-up' hook presentation doesn't seem to be a problem when it comes to securing a hold.

The jig heads, which you can buy or make yourself, may be dressed with fur, feather, buck tail or slinky fibre, as in the case of the pike flies, or may be used with one of the many rubber worms that are widely available, and cheap and easy to replace when they become too damaged.

METHODS AND TECHNIQUES

Whether boat or bank fishing, it is obviously important to operate where the fish are, and as far as possible waste as little time as you can where they are not! Naturally the pike may be anywhere, but there are many obvious places where you can expect them to be. For example, in large lakes and reservoirs, a good general rule would be to concentrate on the shallows and margins in the early spring and autumn, and if you fish through the late spring and summer, expect them to have retreated to the deeper water. In mid-winter they could be anywhere!

Our Midland gravel pits tend to be between six and twelve feet (two to four metres) in depth, which seems to suit the pike well in all seasons. My approach is to cover the water as extensively as possible: 'Show 'em it and move on!' I am not one to stay in any one spot for long, trying different lures, unless I happen to have come across what Tim and I call a 'nest' of pike. I choose what fly or lure is a good bet for the conditions, and then try to show it to as many pike as I can. We find that they are either 'up for it' or not, and the strange thing is that they all seem to understand which it is to be! Having said that, it is always worth persevering, because even on the most unlikely dour days, there just might be a 'village idiot' fish somewhere, and it could be the big one you've been praying for.

In the river we have found that there are stretches with very few pike in them, and others where they are almost always in residence. I presume that they are never going to be too far away from their food, and therefore if you can find the bait fish you have found the key to success. Weir pools are almost always great places to try, as are back streams, points where back streams and the main river meet, slacks below bends, and anywhere you find a small side stream or ditch joining the river. Other than these types of location, it is simply a matter of fishing methodically down stretches of bank, and inevitably you will soon be able to build up a picture of the 'hot spots'. I do enjoy this type of mobile angling: there is always a new place to try, something new to look at, and you never know what may be round that next bend!

When fly fishing there are two basic approaches: first, fish a line that will present the fly at a depth of three to six feet (one to two metres) from the bottom, whilst retrieving at an appropriate speed. My local River Nene is about six to ten feet (two to three metres) deep in general, and in clear water conditions (which are *essential*, as I have mentioned earlier) I find the slow-sink (or 'slime line') to be the most

useful. In the shallower reaches it may be necessary to commence the retrieve as soon as the fly hits the surface, whilst in the deeper sections I tend to wait a few seconds to allow the fly to sink – I 'count it down' – before working it back. I usually cast square across the river, hopefully within a foot or two of the far bank/reeds, then take two or three paces downstream before starting the retrieve. This is a good way to get the fly down a bit, and at the same time cover the water and work steadily down the stretch.

The second method can be used in any depth of water, and uses a very fast sinking line, a short leader (two to four feet/90cm to a metre), and a lure incorporating a Plastazote buoyant head – the classic 'booby' or 'ballydoolagh bomber' effect, as promoted by that well-known Irish fly-piker Alan Hanna.

The 'fly' is constantly trying to rise 'head first', whilst the line is lying along the bottom, and each pull causes the fly to dive. The action is therefore an 'up-and-down' wiggle, and can be deadly at times, and the motion and distance from the lake/river bed is varied with the leader length and retrieve speed.

When 'spinning' or jerking I try to cover the water in the same way, that is, two or three paces between casts, and thus literally miles of bank can be fished in the course of a day: the more fish you cover, the better your chance of a good catch. Lakes and gravel pits can be approached in the same way: that is, by working steadily along the shore. I never cast in the same place twice unless there is a special reason to do so – for instance, if I have had a pull or follow, or know the location to be a 'hot-spot'. Similarly, if a pike follows the lure or fly 'lazily' at a distance of three feet (a metre) or more, the chances are that it won't take even if you have another fifty throws at it. I know there are always exceptions, but unless they chase really close, or 'flash' at the lure, or look very excited, I just move on to find another customer. The fish that are really 'up for it' will be on to your offering instantly – far too fast, in fact, for you to get it away from them!

Boats

The use of a boat can be a real asset and will greatly increase your chances of success, giving you access to areas that cannot be fished from the shore. In addition it enables you to take both fly *and* jerk outfits, something I find impractical when on foot, and it also widens your options with regard to fishing techniques: anchoring, drifting and back-drifting.

Anchoring

Positioning the boat in a hot spot near an island or downwind shore can be a good ploy, fanning your casts in all directions until the area has been adequately covered. For myself, I am never happy to be long in one place, but it is a simple matter to lift the anchor and reposition in the next likely looking spot.

Drifting

Depending on the wind strength, the idea here is to drift downwind, bows first, with one angler casting left and the other right. With fly or jerk this covers a huge amount of water, every cast being in a fresh place. Another big plus for this technique is that as the lure is retrieved, the boat is steadily moving, which means there is a 'round the bend' effect, which is often deadly. The motion of the boat can be 'trimmed', either with an electric motor, or drogue, or both, and in this way a whole lake or pit can be systematically worked. In relatively light winds, the boat may be steered by rudder in and out of bays at the desired distance from the shore, or a small electric motor can be employed to achieve the same. The big advantage of the motor is that it becomes a simple matter to work along the downwind shore (often the place to be), thirty or forty yards out, and casting in towards the bank.

Back Drifting

This is another invaluable technique, useful for flies or lures, and in any depth of water. Basically the boat is allowed to drift ('side-on' this time), with or without the use of a drogue, and the anglers cast upwind. Line may be paid out if required, and then retrieved appropriately to present the bait at the desired speed and depth, and so on.

This method is ideal for fishing the buoyant fly/lead line combination, enabling large areas of the lake bed to be covered with the fly working just off the bottom – deadly for pike, perch and zander, if present. If you possess a depth-finder, it is possible to enjoy the great benefit of seeing the depth, snags and even fish, before your flies cover the area, and this can be both useful and very exciting in the relatively deep water of a reservoir. Bob and I had a couple of successful and very enjoyable trips to Grafham last season, fishing as described above, and we boated some pristine pike and really 'classy' perch.

Fly Casting

I am not sure that I should attempt to explain the technique of actually casting a fly; it's much easier to watch someone who can do it, or watch a video of the same, or perhaps even book a lesson with a qualified casting instructor. Nevertheless, I could maybe offer just a couple of pointers to success.

Firstly, remember that the line will inevitably follow the path of the rod *tip*,

and therefore the 'round-the-clock' action, quite suitable for lure casting, is *hopeless* for throwing out a fly! It is essential to try to keep the tip ring of the rod moving back and forth in as straight and horizontal a plane as is possible; it then acts just like a catapult, throwing the line well back in the air, for without a good back cast there is no way you will achieve a decent forward one!

Secondly, the technique known as 'double-hauling' is strongly advised if you are ever to cast any sort of distance, and this basically involves a smooth progressive pull with the left (non rod-holding) hand, both on the back cast and then again on the forward one. In between, the left hand feeds the line back up towards the first ring, ready for the second pull. The idea is to 'load' the rod (that is, bend it more), which greatly increases the line speed and therefore distance. If that all sounds a bit complicated, don't be put off! It's really quite simple, and so satisfying to see the result!

Striking (Setting the Hook)

As I have mentioned several times, there are occasions when the pike are aggressively 'in the mood', and when this is the case, hooking them is no problem: the fly is in the scissors, tongue or gill-rakers, and that, basically, is that. However, you will certainly experience many occasions when the fly (or lure) stops suddenly and a fish is on, then just as quickly is off again. I believe this to happen when the pike is just curious, or half interested, and simply clamps its powerful jaws on to your offering. Such is the power of those jaws, that at that stage you could strike with a telephone pole without having any effect on the fly. Then, having decided that it doesn't really want to eat it after all, the fish just opens its mouth and ejects the hook. It never was really 'on', simply holding the bait with a grip like a vice. Unfortunately, on these

---

Easy when you can do it...

Having said that it just may be a question of 'It's easy when you can do it!'. In the last few days I tried to teach an old college friend, whom I hadn't seen for decades, to cast a spinning rod and fixed-spool reel. This fellow is a talented, sensible, bright and internationally famous SCUBA diver and photographer, but his initial attempts were so inept that I simply could not believe it! Rather unkindly, I ended up rolling around on the ground giggling uncontrollably, much to his consternation – I never was much of a teacher! He did eventually catch a pike, I am pleased to report, *much* to my relief!

---

occasions it tends to happen repeatedly – that is, *all* the fish seem to be in the same investigative mood. I don't think there is much we can do in these circumstances, but my general advice is firstly, to maintain a really tight line, and then give two or three firm strikes in the hope that if/when the pike tries to eject the bait, the hook catches somewhere suitable *on its way out*. At the end of the day I think it's a case of 'some you win, some you lose'!

THE FUTURE

What are the piking prospects for the coming years? On the plus side, certainly in my area, more and more new gravel pits are constantly being excavated, and every new one is a potential future pike venue. Also the rivers are definitely cleaner than they were in my youth, and that has to be good, both for wildlife and fish. When I was a youngster it was really something to see a kingfisher, but these days I see at least one on nineteen out of twenty trips, which must be another good sign, for sure.

LEFT & OPPOSITE: The two twenty-pounders fly caught from Grafham in October 2005.

Trout fisheries, whilst not quite so popular as they have been in the past, are still patronized by many anglers, and we all know how well pike grow on a part rainbow diet! At the same time, I think that most people acknowledge that pike also thrive on neglect, in that the more they are fished for, the worse they seem to do – and here I am helping to promote the sport and encourage even more people to take up this increasingly popular pastime!

However, let us hope that there will be enough fishing for all of us. As I have mentioned previously, we are certainly well blessed with venues here in the Midlands, so I feel fairly confident of the chance of decent sport for at least the rest of *my* days!

As for techniques, I am fairly sure that fly fishing for coarse fish is going to be the way forward. Pike, perch, zander, chub, big rudd and even bream and carp have, at various times, fallen for the charms of my

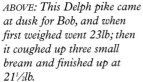

ABOVE: This Delph pike came at dusk for Bob, and when first weighed went 23lb; then it coughed up three small bream and finished up at 21½lb.

TOP RIGHT: John Emerson, Bob's partner at Grafham when they both hooked pike over 30lb together. Bob's unfortunately escaped, but not before they had seen it. John's went 30½lb; Bob's looked even bigger. This was a very rare incident.

CENTRE RIGHT: With his very next cast he hooked this monster twenty-nine-pounder with the same method.

Trolled livebait caught this fish for Bob when all else failed, on a freezing cold January day in 2003. It went 26lb 12oz.

ABOVE: An old-fashioned way of keeping pike. With care, no harm came to them. The best is 20lb-plus.

LEFT: A traditional yet efficient livebait bucket, now a collector's item.

BELOW: Lures available in the 1950s, still effective on their day, from the left: metal minnow; rubber wagtail; simple Norwich spoon; mackerel spinner; two Colorado spinners/spoons; copper Norwich; blue and silver Vibro (not made today); a kidney spoon with red inside blade; and on the top, an Ondex barspoon and a simple, jointed, early plastic plug.

ABOVE: Old-fashioned Fenland setlines, confiscated by the author; standard gaff (now outlawed); safety-point gaff (which did not really work); tube-and-slit disgorger, now replaced by forceps; long-nosed pliers; and hook cutters.

BELOW: Gags, three shown closed, one in operating gape, and one protected by tape. These are inefficient tools, now rapidly declining in use.

BELOW: Early floats, not much used today, mostly Fishing Gazette style (with slit and peg); small slider or pilot floats; early plastic moveable floats (with incorrect streamlining!); top centre is a Dennis Pye dumbbell float; bottom left is a wooden slider from the early 1900s that needed a peg, but had no slit; second right, bottom row is a Bill Winship controller-cum-sinker float, attached by rubbers top and bottom.

ABOVE: *A small selection of modern lures: to the left, in rubber (very popular in the mid-2000s); a copper and silver Lucky Strike Lizard (on which the author caught over 800lb of pike in a day and a half); below the Lizard is a Barrie's Buzzer Spinnerbait (which may have revolutionized lure fishing); then two Super Shad Raps separated by a small, lurid spoon, sometimes an absolute killer; a large green and yellow jerkbait; a neutral depth crankbait (that is, a floating diver); a 'trouty' rubber arrangement with a large waggly tail. The bottom two are a Crazy Crawler, the grandfather of surface action lures; and a small crankbait.*

ABOVE: *Super Shad Rap, shown heavily tangled in the netting of a landing net. Yet with this netting material it can be removed in ten seconds (unlike micromesh netting that could take at least ten minutes).*

TOP: *Selection of more modern floats: second from the left is a depth finder with its crook of plastic tube at the top; third left is a groundbait feed float ideal for adding fishy smells to the swim; third right is a transparent float (incorrectly streamlined); second right is a self-cocker (to be used with caution only at the exact depth). Note that the stubby float in the top row is a rebuilt* Fishing Gazette *float with the slit filled and the streamline taper correct.*

ABOVE: *Tim Cole and Barrie Rickards about to load gear for a few days' piking in Fenland.*

MIDDLE: *Reels used up until the 1950s: top left, Alcock's Aerial (still used by Barrie Rickards); the second black reel is a Rapidex (that the author occasionally uses); the fixed-spool reels are Omnia, one with a full bale arm and the other with a half or flying-spike bale arm (both used in the 1950s by the author); three wooden starbacks (note the working repair on the largest of these).*

RIGHT: *A big fish from the Great Ouse.*

Bob was given a 'copper'-painted jerkbait, which on its first outing accounted for 90lb of pike, including this twenty-one-pounder.

ABOVE: *M. G. pike flies tied as described in the text on 5/0 Aberdeen hooks.*

LEFT: *A fine catch of pike, all on spoon. Ron Randall is the angler who found that a very fast retrieve with silver spoon was what they wanted. The reason for retaining them was that they were moved into an adjoining pit, alive and well.*

ABOVE: Good medicine for pike! – Left column: top 4; Standard 6–7in M.G. type pike flies. Bottom 3; Buoyant-headed fry imitations. Middle column: top 4; M.G. home-made jerkbaits. Bottom Luhr-Jenson 'fingerling' crankbait. Right column: top to bottom; Standard 'Ondex', M.G. 'Giant Ondex', Rebel J 30, Storm-jointed Thunderstick, Big S Plug, plus three 'jigbaits'.

RIGHT: I look fairly pleased with this jerk-caught pike of 24lb 6oz from a gravel pit.

BELOW: A beautifully marked, fly-caught fish from a Bedfordshire gravel pit.

A wild Irish Lough pike of 29lb 4oz that fell to a smelt.

ABOVE: A tiny bit of prebaiting two days earlier produced this Fenland 29lb 7oz.

A nice one from Pitsford reservoir.

BELOW: *Broadland rivers such as the Bure are excellent deadbait waters. This mid-double took a smelt.*

ABOVE: Location is important when deadbaiting. This Irish river pike of 20lb 2oz came from under an overhanging tree.

BELOW: A Lomond twenty in a rainstorm.

Nige Williams with a nice Windermere pike, one of the north-west waters where livebaits and many types of deadbait are banned.

BELOW: A big Esthwaite pike of 20lb plus!

A brace of 25lb-plus pike: 25lb 12oz and 25lb 4oz.

LEFT: Gord Burton the 'Pirate' with a big one.

CENTRE: A super windy twenty-pounder: 27lb 8oz.

RIGHT: A tremendous battler of almost 30lb.

flies (and not always pike flies), and as far as pike are concerned, on the right days they just can't get on quick enough!

This last season (2004) has about run its course now. I was lucky enough to land four twenty-pounders over the winter, one on livebait, one on a home-made jerkbait, and two on fly, including a very fit-looking 22lb fish from my local River Nene three weeks ago. Unfortunately I was on my own at the time (I wish Bob would retire!), and so had to photograph the fish lying next to the rod, which is never quite the same.

Whilst I would always choose to retain my options to fish live- or deadbaits whenever I wish, or feel that they would, in the circumstances, give me the best chance, I would definitely encourage all pikers to give artificials a thorough try – I very much doubt if you will be disappointed!

STOP PRESS

I know I am becoming even more fanatical about the fly-fishing side of predator angling, and I have had some spectacular results. In the autumn of 2005 I ended my carping sessions with half an hour of casting surface flies around the shallows, taking pike up to 12lb. Bob and I also tried bottom-hugging flies on the reservoirs in twenty to thirty feet (six to ten metres) of water; and although it was fairly slow going at times, the rewards were sometimes worth it. I was lucky enough to notch up two immaculate 20lb-plus pike (in mid-October 2005), and was delighted with a bonus of two zander of 8 and 9lb. What a great start to the 2005 winter season that was!

4. Catching Pike on Live- and Deadbaits

by Neville Fickling

The roach angler will catch well on bread, while the majority of carp anglers fish with baits that resemble nothing they could ever find in the wild. Modern coarse fish baits can range from sweetcorn to luncheon meat, and even the humble maggot, the larvae of a *terrestrial* insect, is a rare natural encounter for our freshwater omnivores.

Predators, and in particular the pike, want to eat fish, and it does not matter whether that fish is live, dead, rotten even, or a reasonable simulation of the real thing. Pike want to eat fish. In one instant our task of catching big pike is immediately made easier – and also harder. So you might think that because pike eat fish, all we need to do is use a fish to catch a pike: nice and simple, which I like. But it gets harder when you consider there are thousands, perhaps millions, of other fish competing with your handful of baits. How do you make yours preferable to the wild offerings? If the pike have been caught many times on the baits you have access to, what can you do to ring the changes? Do we try sausages or pork chops, or is that just a little too outlandish to work? In actual fact we have to return to fish baits for pike, because fish or their imitations are the only baits that consistently catch pike. Perhaps something will come along in the future, but until then for most of the time it's live- and deadbaits as first choice.

I have always been a great believer in using both live- and deadbaits whenever

possible. There are situations where one method will be better than the other, but overall in most situations it is sensible to use both approaches. My own results reflect this dual approach. The last time I did a count, roughly two-thirds of my bait-caught pike fell to deadbaits, while the rest fell to livebaits. Now, whether or not this is a true reflection of the preferences of the pike I fish for, or a function of how I fish for them, I'm not sure. Certainly other successful pike anglers catch a much bigger percentage of their pike on livebaits, but that is because they choose to livebait as a first choice wherever they go. Similarly I know pike anglers who never livebait, and catch all their pike with deadbaits and also of course lures. (Lure fishing falls outside my brief here.)

Livebaiting as a method requires the most effort and is most likely to see the angler fall foul of the law of the land; also, in the face of poorly informed opinion, it is used as the first line of attack by those who would like to see angling banned. Never one to shirk my responsibilities, I shall deal with livebaiting first.

LIVE- AND DEADBAITING SUMMER OR WINTER?

There are so many other species to fish for that not many pike anglers fish all the year round for pike. Generally lure fishing is

Fishing for big pike can take the angler to some spectacular places. Lough Nafooey in Mayo, Ireland.

probably the best approach if you are going to summer fish; it is certainly a lot easier than livebaiting. Livebaits tend to be very difficult to keep alive in the summer, and really the pike fishing has to be wonderful for me, at any rate, to bother. Deadbaits are a different matter and certainly you can do well using them in the summer. Unfortunately eels can be a big nuisance in the summer, and sometimes you have to keep to fairly eel-proof baits such as lamprey or eel sections. Mackerel and herring are frequently torn to pieces by eels, and

unless you like reeling in a 2lb eel tangled to death by your trace and line, then avoid these two as bait!

Some waters have trends. I remember on the Thurne there would be periods, such as the autumn, when deadbaits were predominant; then in the depths of winter livebaiting would become more successful. But such trends are seldom permanent: if they were, it would make life much easier. However, it pays to try and spot these trends, because if you are fishing three rods you can then either fish two rods with lives

The keen angler is always at the water before dawn.

and one with a deadbait, or vice versa depending on the pike's preference. I always say this, but where you can fish lives and deads do not forsake one or the other.

LIVEBAITING

The Arguments 'For' and 'Against'

First it would be worthwhile considering the arguments for and against livebaiting.

Those who are against it maintain that:

- it is cruel;
- fish diseases can be spread from water to water;
- if anglers do not livebait, the 'antis' will leave us alone, or at least not pay us as much attention.

Before I give the case in favour of livebaiting I have to respond to the points above.

The cruelty issue is not that easy to dispose of, except it must be seen that life as a

A livebait-caught twenty.

member of the animal kingdom itself is inherently cruel. Animals eat each other as a matter of course. The majority of human beings eat meat, and in order to do this some animal has to die. While great efforts are taken to make the death of an animal such as a cow less cruel, who are we to know that a cow does not feel intense mental anguish prior to being despatched in the abattoir?

The fact is that we simply do not know. A roach that has been grabbed by a pike and has incurred a series of deep slashes or perforations to its body will attempt to escape because it is instinctively aware that being grabbed and eaten is undesirable from the point of view of perpetuating its own genes. The fact that some heavily damaged roach do escape and then recover enough to start feeding again suggests that physical damage, provided it is not too extensive, certainly does not produce pain as we know it, otherwise a fish would probably not feed again. There are numerous examples of fish that have been terribly damaged, but which still feed. I suspect if you or I had part of our intestines showing through our body cavity we would not be inclined to feed very much.

All the evidence is that fish do not feel pain as we know it. Almost certainly there are sensory cells dotted about a fish which will tell it that it has been damaged, but this is purely for self-preservation, and encourages the animal to avoid such unfavourable stimulation, by attempting to escape from the cause. In higher animals the same certainly applies, with the addition of much longer-lasting pain, probably there to tell you not to move the leg otherwise you'll damage it even more. This is not scientific, but when you catch a small fish it wriggles to get off the hook, and as soon as you release it, it swims off: there is no behaviour that I can see here to suggest that it is in pain. Indeed, when the 5lb pike came back for the same bait for the third time, I would suggest that aversion therapy does not work for pike, at least.

As regards fish diseases spreading from one water to another, there are no cases that I can think of where this has happened in recent years. Indeed, I think our Environment Agency would be hard pressed to come up with any concrete evidence. I am sure it is possible, but at the same time it should be noted that more suspect fish are moved around by dishonest fish dealers than by pike anglers. While it is true that some non-native fish can become established where they are not wanted, our friend the fish dealer can be just as much to blame: witness the accidental introduction of ide to some Yorkshire rivers.

As for the 'antis', well, we could try to appease them by giving up the right to livebait, and next they will turn their attention to keepnets. Then it will be maggots and worms, and once they have progressed this far we might as well pack in fishing altogether.

Legality

Let's now look at the legality of livebaiting in Britain and some European countries. It is certainly illegal in Eire, Northern Ireland, Germany and Holland; in Germany the Green party has seen to this. In Northern Ireland and Eire livebaiting was banned to stop the spread of roach – which, I might say, it has singularly failed to do! In England, Wales, Scotland, Sweden and Norway you can still livebait, and of course in France there would be blockades in the street if anyone tried to interfere with the Gallic fisherman's right to fish with livebait. For the most part then, we are concerned with England, Wales and Scotland.

Scotland, as I write, is still a free-for-all with no legislation that I know about concerning the unregulated movement of live-baits. This does not mean that the authorities have not been vociferous in their attempts to discourage the movement of fish. This is entirely understandable as rare fish populations and waters with unique ecologies need to be protected. Sadly in many cases, such as that of Loch Lomond, alien fish introductions have already occurred. Some would like to blame pike anglers for all the introductions, but there are also those who would seek to fish for species not previously present in waters such as Lomond. It does not take much effort and certainly little risk to move a dustbin full of chub from the River Ribble to Loch Lomond. As I write this the writing would appear to be on the wall for live-baiting in Scotland, even though banning it will not do anything to reverse what has already happened.

In England and Wales you have to have what is known as 'Section 30 consent' to move fish from one water to another, and all pike anglers who wish to livebait using baits caught from another water should seek to obtain such consent. I have managed to get it in certain circumstances, so it is worth trying to do things legitimately. Otherwise you have to catch the bait from where you are fishing. On some waters this is fairly straight forward, on others nearly impossible. There are some areas in England where you cannot livebait at all, notably the majority of the lakes in the Lake District. Legislation was brought in to protect rare species such as vendace and arctic char from the consequences of the introduction of non-native species. While I can sympathize with this, it doesn't do anything to stop Mr and Mrs Bloggs letting their pet carp, goldfish or channel catfish go once they have outgrown their tank! Sadly, society is so poorly informed about our wildlife that the Draconian legislation brought in by the EA will at best postpone the inevitable.

Sourcing and Keeping Bait

Having got the legal niceties out of the way, how do you organize yourself to live-bait effectively? Well, some of us are lucky. For instance, I have a number of carp-fishing lakes and a stock pond from which I can catch plenty of rudd and roach baits. Other anglers have to do as I used to do, and that is either catch them from club or public waters, or buy them from a fish farm. But before you raid your local club's water, consider this; many clubs pay a lot of money to restock their waters, so is it really fair to help yourself? My preference would be to go to a fish farm and buy small carp, roach or rainbow trout. In this way no one loses, and your conscience will be clear.

Once you've sourced your bait, you need to keep them. A 50gal (225ltr) minimum tank is required (some header tanks are suitable, but sometimes it is easier to get one made). This has to have either a through-flow of clean water or a recirculation system to keep the water clean. Standard Koi pond technology is all that is required for the tanks and plumbing. The most expensive part will probably be the pump to circulate the water, as it involves a settling tank and a filter tank, though it can all be done on the cheap if you shop around. Aeration is also essential, and can be supplied by a good quality mains aerator. If you can keep your livebait tank indoors it avoids the problem of freezing in winter, and it is also much easier to gather the baits together in the morning if you have plenty of light and it isn't pouring with rain.

Regarding the types of fish you might keep, some species will survive well in warm weather, particularly carp, crucian carp and rudd. Other species, such as perch and roach, survive better once the water temperature drops below 10°C.

Though easy to maintain once the water temperature is under 10°C, trout need a little care when it comes to keeping the water clean; but provided you do this (it is ammonia from waste products that causes the problem) they can be kept for months, and with a small amount of food can even grow!

To get your baits from A to B you will need a nice big 4 to 5gal (20 to 25ltr) bucket with a tight-fitting lid, along with a powerful 12V aerator. I favour the 'Power Bubbles', which is the best 12V aerator I have come across so far. For retention at the water a bait tube or a bait cage is useful, the cage being best for tough species such as carp and trout, and the tube for other, more fragile species.

Techniques

The Paternoster Rig

Livebaiting techniques depend on whether you know the pike are in a limited area, or you need to search for them. The sunken float paternoster rig is the favoured approach for fishing a known swim or area. It doesn't work very well in weedy or really shallow water of under three feet (a metre), but once you have a decent depth or reasonably weed-free water, you are in business. There are many versions of the basic rig, but the one I have shown works well in the autumn and winter.

In the warmer months care has to be taken with any paternoster, because bait activity can cause tangles. Certain species such as rudd and silver bream are great tanglers, while crucian carp and perch cause few problems. If you are attentive while fishing you will soon spot the problem species, and there are ways to minimize these problems – one that I favour is to mount the baits tail down on the trace. Normally I'd mount a livebait with one hook in the dorsal root and another in the

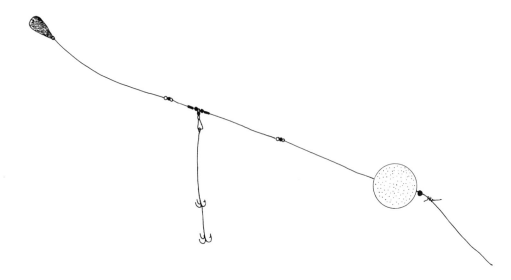

Sunken float paternoster.

pectoral root. However, the tail-up presentation with one hook in the tail root and the other in the pectoral root forces the bait to swim against the resistance of the tackle, and in so doing avoids tangling.

The action from this presentation is obviously different from the conventional paternoster presentation, which is mainly round and round. What induces a pike to strike a paternostered livebait is not immediately obvious, because the action is hardly natural. However, pike are not possessed of great thinking powers, and if a tethered meal presents itself for long enough near to a pike, there is a good chance it will take it. Exceptions do occur, and these can be associated with previous captures. Though pike are not particularly bright, they do show a degree of suspicion if they have been caught on a particular presentation recently.

Free-swimming Bait

If you have any doubts about the efficiency of a paternostered bait, you have to consider a free-swimming bait. This simply entails using a bait fished under a float and allowed to swim around your swim. While this presents a bait in a more natural manner, it does involve recasting, particularly if the wind is not favourable (that is, the wind is blowing from the side, or towards you). This inevitably means that more baits are required, something that causes problems when they are in short supply. The free-swimming bait with the wind behind you can be used to search out an area. Change the conventional float for a drifter, and it is quite easy to cover even greater areas, including those out of casting range. While the normal dorsal/pectoral root mounting is fine for short-range work, drifting is better performed with the bait head up the trace. This entails hooking the bait through the top lip with the top treble, and placing the second treble in the dorsal root. Mounted in this way a bait is pulled through the water in as natural a manner as possible. On the retrieve the bait comes in easily and is not overtired, which would

Everything is returned alive these days.

happen if it were retrieved in any other manner. There is also the chance on a slow retrieve of inducing a take as you wind in. I should also mention that when using the float paternoster on rivers, it is a wise idea to mount the bait head up the trace, otherwise the water pressure will exhaust the bait and also tend to pull it into the side, unless you use a ton of lead.

Ledgering

Ledgered livebaits are not used very much these days for pike, which is a shame, because this is an effective technique. The problem today on many waters is that weed growth is often heavy, and this makes a ledgered livebait ineffective, the bait often tending to bury itself in the weed. You can get around this to some extent by attaching a Fox-bait popper to one of the trebles, and by doing this the livebait can still work effectively over the top of the weed. Obviously in very dense weed you are fighting a losing battle. For ledgering livebaits, baits can be mounted head up the trace, which results in a bait that tends to spend much of its time resting on the bottom. Mounted tail up the trace, the bait spends more time trying to swim against the running lead placed on the line.

Trolling

Some waters require a highly mobile approach, and here trolling is required. Now we are entering into the realm of boat fishing. While not wishing to write a chapter on boat fishing here, there are certain key things I would say. If you choose to boat fish, go for the biggest boat you can launch and tow. Don't go for the 'small

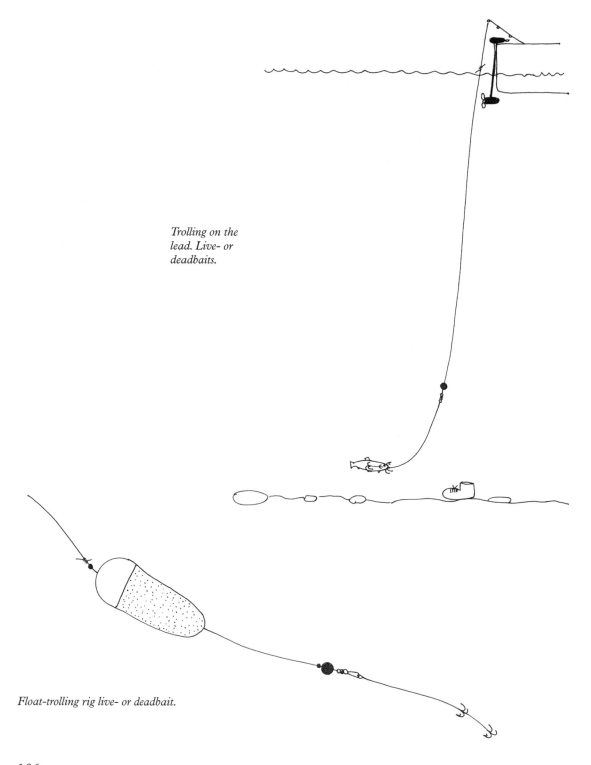

Trolling on the lead. Live- or deadbaits.

Float-trolling rig live- or deadbait.

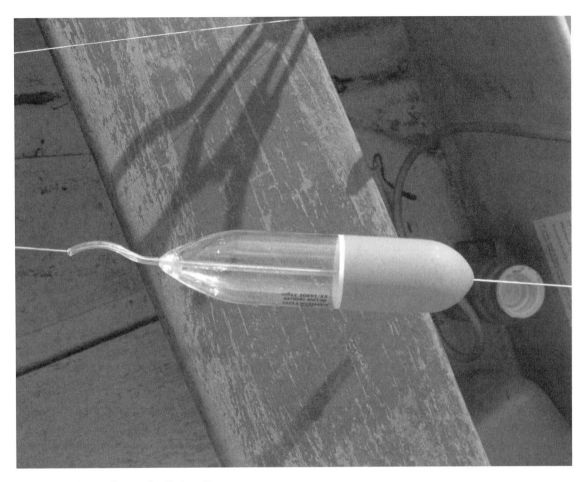

Fox-trolling float or live- or deadbait trolling.

boat will do for me' strategy, because sooner or later you'll have a fright and you'll wish you had taken my advice.

Most livebait trolling requires the use of an electric motor, though in some situations you may be forced to row, or in some cases may decide that rowing is a more effective way of presenting your baits. I'm perfectly happy always to use my electric motor, mainly because I usually fish alone, and tending rods as well as rowing can be a nightmare. Standard trolling kit is a Minn Kota electric motor. Most people use a

55lb thrust unit, and it is essential to have one with stepless control. Cheaper models lack this, and it really is difficult to troll effectively without a variable speed control. To troll effectively you'll also need an echo sounder, not to find the fish, but to maintain an idea of the depth.

Generally if I am fishing alone in the boat on a water with a reasonably clean bottom, I will opt to float-troll one livebait, and fish another directly over the back of the boat using a lead without a float. If the water is very snaggy, such as Ladybower, then direct over the back of the boat is a recipe for disaster. I remember having a day on Ladybower with Nige Williams. He tried to fish a bait near the bottom without a float, but by mid-morning, having snagged up umpteen times, he decided to give it best. The reason for using the float-fished and on-the-lead livebait together is that they present the bait in a different manner: the float-fished bait can fish deep, but generally it tends to ride up higher in the water than the lead-only bait.

The lead-only bait fishes very close to the bottom, provided you go slow enough; this really can make a difference on some waters. I can think of a number of trout waters (most of which are now defunct) which saw the pike down deep: Weirwood was one, as still is Grafham Water. On the other hand, Esthwaite up in the Lake District has always had a reputation as a water where the takes you get come to relatively shallow-fished baits.

With each new water you approach it is vital to try where the situation allows the two basic trolling approaches, otherwise you may well find yourself missing out. As far as the techniques are concerned, everything is fairly simple. Baits are mounted head up the trace, and on trout livebaits or around 4oz (113g) I use two size 2 Gamakatsus. These allow an instant strike, and by 'instant' I mean exactly that: you get the take, stop the motor, stand up, wind down, and bend into it hard. If you miss it with a bait that size and two size 2 hooks, then it either wasn't really interested or it was too small anyway. At the moment the chances to use float-trolled livebaits are very limited because there are few trout waters where you can do it legitimately. There are also absurd rules regarding electric motor trolling on Broadland waters, despite the Environment Agency having relaxed its 'no motor trolling' byelaw.

Bait Size

One subject generates more heat when dealing with livebaiting, and that is bait size. We know that pike are quite capable of eating prey fish of a third their own size, sometimes larger. This should not, however, encourage us to use 10lb pike live-baits to catch thirty-pounders! There has to be a sensible limit to the size of livebaits that can be used: the bigger the bait, generally the more problems you'll have hooking the pike. Usually most pike anglers accept that the realistic upper weight of a livebait is around 12oz (340g), though of course on occasions people have used 1lb roach and 2lb chub as bait.

I am totally against banning anything in angling unless it can be shown to be bad for the fish we fish for. However, care has to be taken not to alienate our fellow coarse anglers by using what to them would be a specimen fish. A 1lb roach is a nice fish to catch, and you can hardly justify not killing pike if you go through a tub full of 1lb roach in a day! There are sensible alternatives, of course. You can buy 8oz to 12oz trout or carp and use these, and there will be little problem because these fish in most cases will be destined for the pot anyway. The only problem with these fish is the Section 30 consent mentioned earlier, and with carp the need to give consideration to the existing stocks of carp in a water. It would be a disaster if an unscrupulous angler used a diseased carp on one of our best carp waters, and it resulted in the death of most of the big carp in the water.

There is little doubt that a big livebait will often get a response from a pike more quickly than a smaller bait. The vibration and visible signals that a big bait sends out are very tempting for any pike, and because they are creatures of instinct they know that one big meal is much more energy

Sometimes you have to sit it out for a run. On a water like this, who cares!

efficient than several smaller ones. If you decide to use a big bait, say a 12oz carp, you may get the take, but you still have to hook it. Hooks have to be much bigger than normal. The minimum size used are size 2s, and though pike can be hooked using just a pair of these, some anglers step up to three of these. Though most of us use semi-barbless trebles, there is the temptation when using big baits to go fully barbed. I'm not altogether happy with this, because should there be a breakage some unfortunate pike may swallow a lot of hooks, which is not going to do it much good.

Personally I feel that big baits just for the sake of big baits are unwise. There needs to be a degree of judgement exercised so that big baits are applied to situations that

warrant them, otherwise a great many inexperienced pike anglers are going to go out and try to emulate their heroes and end up losing fish, losing hooks and annoying anglers who resent seeing 'their' specimen fish being used for bait.

A few years ago I managed to get permission to fish Ladybower reservoir for pike, and Nige Williams and I never used baits bigger than about 6oz (170g) – and usually they were smaller than that, perhaps only 2 to 4oz (56–113g). We caught loads of pike including big ones, simply because we had no competition from other anglers, and small baits would catch any fish we put a bait in front of. This is obviously not always the case, but most anglers do not face really intense competition from other pike anglers, so modest baits will catch the pike in most waters. Perhaps sometimes you have to wait a little longer, but you will catch them eventually. Livebaits are not, of course, the ultimate in pike fishing, and a lot of pike can be caught using deadbaits – indeed, sometimes more pike can be caught on deads; but that is something I will deal with later.

Observing the Rules

For the pike angler who cares not whom he upsets, then using livebaits where they are not allowed can be a short cut to success.

My view in this is that it is up to the individual. I have always tried to keep within the rules, but there have been several situations where other anglers have been breaking the rules and catching big fish. Clubs that operate livebait bans seldom have the means to enforce them, and this inevitably leads to people breaking the rules, and these then have an advantage over those who keep to the rules. It is all rather sad that pike fishing has to end up like this, but these are the facts. Until clubs either allow all legitimate methods or enforce their rules, the whole situation will be a fiasco.

Safely in the net: a mid-double.

DEADBAITING

With a few exceptions, deadbaiting does not present legal problems to the pike angler. The exceptions are these: first, in the Lake District of England the North-West Region of the Environment Agency has banned a number of deadbaits in a somewhat late attempt to stop the spread of alien fish species. These include coarse fish, trout, pollan and any freshwater fish species that might be taken alive to these waters. The theory behind the ban is that some unscrupulous pike angler might take livebaits with him and then as the bailiffs head towards him, kill his livebaits and then be in the clear because they are now deadbaits. They forget that the first instinctive reaction of the persecuted pike angler is to throw the incriminating baits over the side, thus removing all the evidence in one easy move!

Sometimes I wonder what I am paying my £40 a year for when I buy my rod licences. The only protection we have for big pike is what we pike anglers have put in place ourselves via riparian owners and angling clubs. The EA has done little to improve pike fishing in England and Wales other than the occasional transfer of unwanted pike to waters where the existing populations have been depleted by natural or man-made disasters. However, I digress!

If you look through fishing books published prior to the 1950s you will not come across any meaningful reference to the use of static deadbaits to catch pike. What you will find are continuous references to catching pike using lures and livebaits. Where deadbaits were used they would invariably be mounted on a spinning flight designed to give some semblance of movement to the bait. I cannot be certain who was first to discover static deadbaiting for pike, but for my money two independent groups of pike anglers stumbled on the method at the same time. The Taylor brothers from Aylesbury in Buckinghamshire discovered that pike would take deadbaits fished on the bottom, and quickly tried herrings because they were readily available. In Norfolk, Bill Giles and Reg Sandys had come to exactly the same conclusion, having left a deadbait they were wobbling over the side of the boat while they had a break. They, too, made the logical jump to using herrings, simply because they were readily available and the right size. It wasn't until Barrie Rickards and Ray Webb came along that the efficacy of static deadbaiting became really widely known. While a few people were writing about the method, most continued to catch pike on lures and livebaits.

With the publication of *Fishing for Big Pike* by Rickards and Webb (1971), it became impossible to escape the fact that deadbaiting was an effective method, and in some situations it was in fact better than both livebaiting and lures. The results spoke for themselves: catches of up to eight or nine 20lb-plus pike in a season; and fish over 30lb mainly on static deadbaits. A few of us on the fringes of all this big pike catching of course wanted some for ourselves, and indeed my first twenty-pounder came in February of 1968 on a float-ledgered herring. There was still a lot to learn about static deadbaiting, but by now we and many others had seen the light and were moving on exploring new aspects of what was eventually to become the most important branch of pike fishing.

Why do Pike Take Deadbaits?

Before I describe the baits and the techniques we have available, let's look at why pike take deadbaits. It is easy to assume that pike are active predators all the time.

111

Whatever the size of pike, unhook it and photograph it on a soft surface or, better still, an unhooking mat.

It is also understandable to think that pike eat mainly live fish. Our problem is that we live above the water so we do not actually see much of what is going on underwater. Fish die every day, because your average roach, perch or rudd probably lives for less than ten years, and they eventually succumb to disease or old age.

Nature's great aquatic clean-up agency is none other than our friend the pike. Dead or dying food fish are therefore a totally natural feature of underwater life, and pike are instinctively aware that food is food whether it is stiff on the bottom, swimming erratically, or belting along at high speed. So we know pike take deadfish in the wild, but what about the waters where hardly any pike are caught on deadbaits? Those that come immediately to mind are our heavily stocked trout waters. On some of these waters, a run on a deadbait is such a rare event as to be remarkable – though one should never, of course, say 'never'. I have seen with my own eyes pike to 20lb caught on deadbaits on Blithfield in the eighties, so it does happen from time to time. Generally, however, on heavily stocked trout waters you might as well fish with no bait, rather than fish exclusively deadbaits. Why is this, then?

Predatory fish are quite simple-minded creatures, though the mechanisms that make them alive are incredibly complex. While we may be a long way from understanding every detail of what makes a living creature alive, the instinctive behaviour of a fish is fairly easy to come to terms with. Pike live to do two basic things: to eat, and to reproduce. The methods a pike uses to feed are instinctive rather than thought out. What stimulates them to feed can be a combination of factors, but movement of the prey fish is very important. In a fishery where fish stocks are very, very high, moving fish are abundant. A pike in such a water is constantly subjected to the stimuli

of moving fish, and because of this the threshold required to elicit a feeding response is correspondingly higher.

I'll try to explain this in human terms. If you were served every day at home with the finest food, you would eventually become blasé about food. To tempt you to eat out, the meal would have to have the promise of a gastronomic delight. You would certainly not be interested in a downward step provided by a pork chop in lumpy gravy.

The gastronomic delight is the newly stocked trout, somewhat disorientated; the fine meals you are blasé about are the hundreds of trout swimming around the water; and the pork chop is the deadbait, soaking more in hope than anything. This scenario can repeat itself on waters heavily stocked with coarse fish. Fortunately it is rare, and on most waters where the food fish are not that abundant a dead fish will be taken regularly. On waters where the pike are hungry, almost anything will be eaten, but in this situation as pike anglers we might as well use deadbaits all the time, thus saving the livebaits for more discerning pike.

Earlier I said that pike respond to stimuli. Livebaits obviously give out visual, vibratory and, to a lesser extent, olfactory signals... What have deadbaits got going for them? Well, they can obviously be seen, and they can certainly be smelt. Static deadbaits lack movement, and there is certainly no vibratory signal coming from a very dead herring. Once a fish dies it starts to undergo a series of changes. Cell membranes cease to be able to contain their contents, the contents of the gut containing digestive secretions start to digest the tissue that once contained them, and bacteria and fungi start their work to return the corpse to the basic elements it was once formed from. The process described results in lots of fluid, and that liquor is

In autumn pike can swallow baits very quickly. If you have to unhook them this way, strike even more quickly.

mainly water soluble. It inevitably seeps out into the water, and as we know, many fish have a well developed sense of smell. A frozen fish probably gives out even more scent. As a dead fish freezes, ice crystals form in the cells, and these, being jagged and sharp, disrupt the cell membranes. This violent process changes the consistency of the fish's flesh: it becomes softer

and probably more permeable. There have been arguments in the past about the virtues of fresh deadbaits against defrosted frozen baits. The only advantage I can see in freshly killed baits such as roach and trout is the fact that they stand up to casting better. A frozen bait once defrosted must send out more scent for a pike to home in to.

Deadbaits in Use

The choice of deadbaits remains restricted to a fairly limited range. We have yet to get to the stage where we are using any amount of exotic baits from abroad. It is true that a few people in the Manchester area have trawled around the local ethnic fish markets and come up with some interesting-looking baits. My opinion is that if you cannot catch a pike with what we already have available, you are not going to catch it, full stop.

I'm going to look here in chronological order at the deadbaits we now use, showing how and when they came into use. I make the assumption that deadbaits were first used in the 1950s. Dead coarse fish were probably the first accidental deadbaits, and there is a whole host of coarse fish we

We use big baits.

can use, some of which are commercially available, others that you'd have to catch yourself.

Prepacked coarse fish deadbaits usually consist of roach, perch and bream. These baits catch plenty of pike, and though perch are rather tough skinned and do not look much in the water (lacking the silvery scales of the other two species), they work fairly well, and I've certainly always had faith in them in the spring when perch have been busy spawning. At this time perch die quite naturally, and this must present the hunting pike with more free meals than at any other time of year. When fishing in spring in Ireland and Scotland I was always happy to fish dead perch on at least one rod. The best fish that fell to a dead perch was a Lough Allen 27lb 14oz. Bream are good baits, appearing bigger for their weight than they actually are, though because of their shape they tend to cast in a rather eccentric manner. Roach, and less often rudd, have caught plenty of pike for me over the years; the best on a rudd was twenty-seven from a Lincolnshire gravel pit.

Other fish species tend to be harder to obtain, but small chub, dace, gudgeon, carp and even ide and asp (I found these in a batch of dead coarse fish from abroad!) will all catch fish. I'm not sure if pike can tell the difference between each of the species of coarse fish; however, if anyone feels that bream are getting him more takes, I'm not going to argue with that.

Herrings became popular deadbaits simply because anglers in the fifties probably struggled to get hold of roach when they most needed them. There must have been some thoughts that pike wouldn't take a herring because it wasn't a natural food item of a British pike; however, the pike soon proved this to be erroneous. Pike are opportunist feeders, and they really are not bright enough to be able to figure out the origins of a food item. The herring soon proved to be a really good pike bait, and has probably caught more pike than any other deadbait. Its attraction is probably in its distinctive oily smell; also herrings are fairly bright and silver. While it was possible to get small- to medium-sized herring from commercial sources in the 1950s, anglers were probably using quite big baits because the herrings you get off a fishmonger's slab tend to be Norwegian herrings and can be great big things. They also tend to have been on ice for a fair time. Most pike anglers tried lobbing these monster pike baits out until someone realized that you could cut them in half, get two baits, and not end up breaking the rod that was casting them!

These days prepacked herrings are the sensible choice, because they are the right size at 5 to 10in (13–25cm). They also tend to be fresher, being either English caught or Baltic herrings. You can recognize them because they tend to be more silvery, and usually have the scales left on them. Once herrings had been used and shown to catch big pike (my biggest was 34lb on a herring head), pike anglers then started to look at other fish on the fishmonger's slab. The first and most obvious fish that was noticed was the sprat. Now sprats are a different species to the herring, and grow nowhere as large. A big sprat will measure around 5 to 6in (13–15cm), though generally you'll be lucky to encounter many this size. The larger sprats tend to come from the south coast, and are available from about August to January. After January, sprats start to arrive from the east coast, and these tend to be much smaller. So if you are going to use sprats for bait, they must be south coast sprats that you freeze for later use, or you buy prepacked baits that will invariably be the larger fish. Sprats will catch plenty of pike, but for most pike anglers they are a bit small. My best pike on a sprat

117

was 22lb, but in spite of this success, I do not use them these days.

I should mention kippers briefly. These are smoked herrings, and they catch pike on many waters, though first you have to tie the two halves together using mono. My best pike on one went 17lb, but I know Alastair Rawlings has had some good twenties using them.

Frequently on the fishmonger's slab next to the herring were mackerel. Now in the sixties the mackerel that were on the slab were frequently great big 1lb-plus fish. I remember borrowing a beach caster rod and multiplier to fish a big mackerel. I caught a 21lb pike, but I'll not pretend that unhooking it wasn't a messy affair by the time I had given it enough time to get the bait well into its mouth. But it didn't take pike anglers such as Martin Gay, Barrie Rickards and Basil Chilvers long to realize that you could cut a big mackerel in half and obtain two good baits. We now take it for granted that a mackerel head or tail is a superb casting bait and a sensible size, and it also catches pike!

Until now, herring has been the most used deadbait, but before long mackerel will supersede it, if my sales of this bait are anything to go by. In addition to half mackerel baits, we now have very small mackerel, miniature versions of the fish we used to see at the fishmonger's. There are generally two species of small mackerel available: the Atlantic mackerel, and the Spanish or chub mackerel. Both will catch pike, the chub mackerel being the slightly softer of the two species. I honestly don't think pike pay much attention to which species is which.

The mackerel is an oily bait, like the herring, and it wasn't long before someone spotted something even oilier on the fishmonger's slab: the sardine (or a pilchard if it's a big sardine). I think I saw Hugh Reynolds using a sardine for the first time in about 1971. He had trotted off to his local fishmonger's, Mac Fisheries, and bought some – and within a short space of time another bait had been added to the pike angler's armoury. The sardine is a very soft bait, and best fished from frozen; you will certainly not get three full-blooded casts from them once they have thawed out. They tend to be about 5 to 6in (12 to 15cm) long, silvery, and send out an amazing scent/oil trail. I've had fish to 26lb on them, but friends of mine have done better than this, with fish to 35lb. I think that if I'm confronted with very coloured water conditions the sardine is always my first choice, simply because of the scent trail.

Interestingly my company obtained some mega sardines from California a few years ago; some of them were a foot long, and they sold and caught well. Unfortunately the importers obviously struggled to sell enough to the British fish-eating public to make it worth importing any more, so for the time being that will be that! Interestingly it is also really the end for the oily sea baits, because there is nothing else that commonly appears on the fishmonger's slab. From time to time when I receive a large batch of sprats to pack there will be the occasional anchovy in amongst them. They are seldom of usable quality, but if I could get some really fresh ones I'm sure they would catch pike. They have an extremely strong smell, and are very oily.

In 1966 I was pike fishing the Great Ouse Relief Channel when a local man, Harry Nelson, showed me his secret pike bait, a smelt. He used to catch these fish from the tidal Ouse at Magdalen on the Saturday, and then fish with them on the Sunday. It was to be a couple of years before I caught my first 20lb pike on one, but I was immediately sold on smelt as a winning pike bait. Today, instead of trailing around the local fishmonger's (they no

A wild Irish Lough pike of 29lb 4oz that fell to a smelt.

longer exist, anyway) looking for the occasional smelt that might turn up on the slab, we simply go to our local tackle shop, or order a delivery by phone. Convenience is the name of the game these days, and ten years ago who would have thought that carp anglers would no longer roll their own bait?

The smelt is a member of a small group of fish that includes the Argentine and the capelin. It is well distributed around the northern hemisphere, and is a sea fish that spends some time in freshwater and has to return to it to breed. Some populations

are totally landlocked, never returning to sea, but these tend never to reach the size that the migratory smelt manages. It is a constant struggle to get hold of decent-sized smelt, and of course they must be fresh enough to still have that distinctive cucumber-type smell.

Now why exactly pike like them so much is not clear. We know that pike, like most predatory fish, eat what is most readily available, and in the spring in some of our tidal rivers you could once find a lot of smelt spawning. Many of the smelt die after their exertions, and surely pike know that they are easy pickings. Interestingly smelt run up rivers after the pike have spawned, so during that period of recovery this extra supply of food is ideal for the pike, who can pack on weight at this time of year.

It is pure speculation, but perhaps pike are instinctively attuned to the smell of the smelt and simply 'know' there is an easy meal going. If there is anything going on here it *must* be instinctive, because pike residing in still waters and which have never seen a smelt, still take them readily. While the oily deadbaits such as the mackerel, herring and sardine tend to be a bit selective as regards size, on some waters smelt will catch large and small pike. My biggest on a smelt weighed 41lb 6oz, and I think I can safely say there's not much chance of beating that on any bait! Some anglers swear by the very biggest smelt, which can run up to nearly a foot long. We have actually had a group of customers order £500 worth of super smelts in one go. They are not doing this because it looks good, but because unfortunately no bait firm can ever get enough of the really big smelt, so demand always outstrips supply. Personally I am happy with anything around 7 to 8in (18–20cm) – which is just as well, because customers always seem to get the last pack of supers in the cold store!

A relative of the smelt, the capelin, was a useful if small bait, but unfortunately we cannot obtain them at the moment. When I did get hold of some I had pike to 15lb on them, and they did have some promise; they were also very cheap. However, they are heavily fished commercially for fish-meal, and interestingly the last time I saw one it was being fed to a sea lion in New York's Central Park!

All manner of trout have been used extensively over the years. The fishmonger's slab was probably the original source, but these would most likely have been rather large because they were for the table. These days, bait companies supply them at around 6 to 7in (15–18cm) long, which is the ideal size. A fair number of deformed trout are also sold to the bait trade, and these catch pike just as well as normal trout. Rainbows are the most readily obtained, and provided they are fresh and have been starved for a couple of days prior to killing, tend to be nice and tough. We can now get golden trout, which are an amazing orange colour. I'm sure they smell no different to normal trout, but they must have some visual benefits. I've not bothered with blue trout because they look very similar to the normal trout.

Brown trout tend to be harder to get hold of, but are generally tougher baits. There is usually a choice of either farmed or wild browns, the wild ones often bigger than the cultivated fish. I tend to use wild browns on the big natural waters of Scotland or Ireland; they will be part of a pike's natural diet, and it does no harm to give them something they eat regularly. (The fact that sometimes the humble mackerel can beat the natural bait just adds to the confusion!) I'd love to get hold of some arctic char or brook trout, because it is always worth a try using a novelty bait. Unfortunately because the brookie is a non-native species the EA are fussy about its introduction into the wild – though why this doesn't apply in the same way to the rainbow trout escapes me.

Another bait similar to trout is the salmon parr or smolt. There is a vast industry farming Atlantic salmon in cages in Scotland. Salmon parr are produced on fish farms in freshwater before they become smolts, and are placed in cages in the sea. In theory these should be perfectly good baits, but unfortunately in Scotland using immature salmon is a serious offence. I have checked the situation in England and Wales and have it from the

Lamprey is still one of the all-time great baits.

head of the Environment Agency that they see no problem with using cultivated salmon parr or smolts. At present some work will have to be done to sort the matter out in Scotland. At the moment my firm does not sell them, but now the legality in England and Wales has been established I fully intend to add them to my bait range – though I suspect they will catch no more pike than trout.

At some time in 1970 I caught a 16lb pike from the Great Ouse Relief Channel, and in its throat was an eel-like fish that I couldn't identify. When I noticed that it didn't have a backbone, but instead a cartilaginous rod, I realized it was a river lamprey or lampern. The fact that large numbers of these parasitic fish ascend our rivers from the sea to spawn means that they are another bonus for our river and drain pike. Rather like the smelt, I felt that pike would instinctively know that these fish were an easy meal; however, getting a supply of them was another thing. Luckily my smelt fisherman came up trumps: he netted eels during the summer, and in the autumn he caught lampreys as they ran up river prior to spawning in the spring. I was soon using these for my own pike fishing, and it didn't take long to catch some big pike on them. The biggest I ended up catching on a lamprey was 30lb 4oz, which is big enough to convince me how good a bait lamprey is.

Once various eel netters realized that the hundreds of pounds of lampreys they were chucking back had a value, the supply problem was solved. Most lamprey are around a foot long, which makes them ideal for using as half baits. The significant fact about lamprey is that they are full of blood: indeed there seems to be no limit to the amount of blood that will leak out of a lamprey section. Because it is water soluble, it is almost guaranteed that pike will home in on the blood scent trail.

Having the same body form as the lamprey, but no relative at all, the eel is perhaps best known as zander bait; nevertheless a lot of serious pike anglers rate eels highly. At the moment there is great concern about eel stocks being in decline. While I have no doubt that eels in some waters have been overfished, in the waters that I run this is definitely not the case; on one of my fisheries I cannot ledger a deadbait at night without being plagued by eels. However, I have never allowed my lakes to be commercially eel fished, which perhaps indicates where the real problem lies. The eels I use and sell are commercially netted fish that were to be sold for food, but some inevitably die, and these are the ones I sell as bait. In this way I am confident that I am not having any impact on eel stocks in the wild. Some people use whole eels up to a foot (30cm) long, others use sections; I'm happy using either, and the best pike I've had on an eel was 22lb.

Although it has eel in the name, the sandeel is no relative to our freshwater eel. There are several different species of sandeel, and the ones that are of interest to pike anglers are the launce, which can get to about 15in (43cm) long, and the large sandeel. All catch pike, though the biggest single problem is getting enough of them. The capture of these fish depends on our having a hot and relatively calm summer. With our weather it is no wonder we struggle! I have not had much chance to use launce sandeels because customers seem to get them before I do. The normal large sandeel, about 7 to 8in (18–20cm) in length, doesn't look much, but it does catch pike. They have no great smell and are certainly not visual, but I've had pike to 23lb on them so they will remain part of my deadbait armoury.

Going back to the oily baits, one that more or less slipped in unnoticed was the horse mackerel. This member of the mackerel family is very tough, not as oily as the real mackerel, but comes in a suitable size of about 6 to 8in (15 to 18cm). I sell a small amount of these every year, and someone out there likes them. Personally I've never got round to using them regularly so I have no significant personal best on them.

Another rarely used bait that catches pike is the garfish. I've had pike to 17lb on them, although there is one snag: you have to cut off the sharp beak, because I'm a bit nervous about allowing pike to swallow something that could perforate their gut wall.

Exotic baits can be worth a try: this is an asp!

One bait that looks completely hopeless is the pouting or whiting. These tend to turn up with herrings. No one sells them commercially, though I sometimes put one in a product we sell called a 'pike pack'. I chucked one out recently, and actually had a run on it. The fact that it was 25lb 8oz and the fishery was particularly hard fished made me think that I'd found a useful change bait, but unfortunately the humble whiting didn't manage to change my life.

I've covered all the most commonly used baits here, but there are obviously many potential deadbaits, some of which are quite exotic. Experimentation does no harm: small grey mullet, for example,

would make a really good bait. I've used red mullets and gurnard, but usually when there have been no pike for a mile! And I've known pike anglers from London try flying fish: the list of baits is endless. The Asian food markets sell a variety of exotic species, and though I've not had the chance to use any of these, I have seen some interesting-looking fish. Some are catfish, others look like a cross between a stone loach and a sandeel.

Once you have a supply of deadbaits, it helps to have some organized way of keeping them. Most pike anglers will have their own freezer dedicated to deadbaits. Unfortunately in my case the wife still manages to sneak in gourmet meals when her own freezer is full up with the same! Usually I manage to rearrange hers, and quickly sneak all this non-fish back to where it belongs. Baits that have been vacuum-packed tend to keep much better and for longer than those stored loose. Generally, though, vacuum-packed baits are much more expensive.

Bulk packs of bait are generally much cheaper, but need some care if they are to last for up to a year. Most domestic freezers run at about minus 18°C, and the cold store I use runs at minus 30°C. The lower the temperature, the slower the rate of evaporation, and this will ultimately cause a bait to dry out – and once this has happened it is very difficult to rehydrate. My loose baits I will either glaze, or wrap individually in clingfilm. Glazing is simply achieved by dunking them in freezing cold water, which gives them a protective coating of ice. Glazed or wrapped loose baits will keep for a year. And if you have to store baits for longer than a year, then you should go fishing more!

I prefer to keep my baits frozen once I'm on the bank, and to do this you need an 8- or 9-quart (9 or 10ltr) coolbox. These are made by Coleman, and if well packed with a freezer block will keep your baits frozen all day in winter and semi-frozen in the summer. I like this size of box because it fits in a rucksack, thus allowing more free hands when you are walking down the bank. I also cast the baits out already frozen. I see no point at all in thawing the baits out first, because in anything but extremely cold waters a bait will thaw out very quickly – not that the pike worry, and most experienced pikers have had baits grabbed while still frozen. By keeping your baits frozen this enables the angler to return unused baits to the freezer. Few of us can afford to waste baits, and keeping them frozen prevents just that.

At the end of the day I never save my old hookbaits, but throw them in, giving the pike a free feed. After a whole day in the water, baits may well be 'washed out' and no longer leaking juices; therefore I use fresh baits at the start of each session. One bit of reuse I will make during the day is if I get a bait back. I would suggest that if the bait was good enough to have just tempted a pike, it will tempt another. If you must use a fresh bait, then at least save the old bait as a back-up should you risk running out of bait. My best-ever day deadbaiting saw me well supplied with bait, but a twenty-four-pike catch – including twenty-two over tens, topped by two twenties to 27lb – meant that I needed to catch several on the same bait; in fact sometimes the landing net would be used to net the discarded bait rather than the pike. Such days do not happen very often, and if I ever did run out of bait I'd get the lure rods out – or perhaps having caught enough pike for a while, I'd go home. Catching twenty-four pike is actually very hard work, particularly where the banks are steep. In an eight-hour day that is one every twenty minutes!

Deadbait choice is important, but as far as catching pike is concerned, where you fish a bait is probably the key factor that leads to pike-fishing success or failure. Provided you have a selection of baits in your coolbox (I usually take between fifteen and twenty baits for a day's fishing) figuring out where to fish is the key. The way you set up your fishing tackle also has a bearing on your success, and you must have due regard for the safety of the pike you catch.

Just as with livebaiting, we set up in such a manner as to allow us to put a bait where the pike are and hopefully keep it there. The two basic static-on-the-bottom methods are straight ledgering and float ledgering. Years ago people fished without any lead on the line, a method known as free-lining. Unfortunately this method gives very poor bite indication, and inevitably can lead to deep hooking. Free-lining is therefore a method best put into the dust-bin of unwanted fishing methods.

In an ideal world I think we'd always ledger our deadbaits. After all, on a tight line, bite indication will be all but instant, and if you use enough lead your bait is going to stay in position even in a fast-flow-ing river. However, ledgering is something you cannot do on a lot of waters these days, as heavy weed growth, snags and rocks all make it extremely inadvisable. Any situation where the line runs through obstructions can at best cause a pike to eject a bait, or at worst see the line cut through. The solution to this problem is to float ledger. It depresses me to see so many people continuing to ledger in circum-stances that place the pike at risk. The dis-

advantage with float ledgering is that it is more difficult to get the line really tight; its big advantage is that it keeps it out of dan-ger. I've been fishing weedy or rugged waters since the mid-seventies, and ever since I switched to float ledgering life has been remarkably trouble free. The advent of modern braids that tend to ride high in the water has also made life easier.

I've shown the two simple set-ups I use for static deadbaiting: one is a simple run-ning ledger, the other a float ledger that can be modified to perform as a sunken float ledger if required. The sunken float ledger is essential on really big waters when casting from the bank. It enables a sunken line to be fished, thus preventing the wind from dragging the bait out of position. There is little doubt that for maximum dis-tance the straight running ledger is the rig to employ, but as I have already men-tioned, the problem of keeping the line

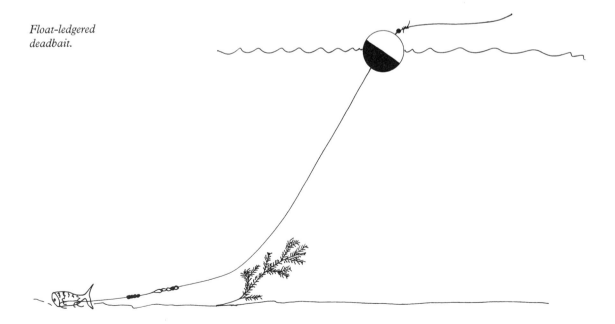

Float-ledgered deadbait.

Basic ledger rig.

clear of rocks and snags can make the takes you get (and then lose) highly priced... If I had to go for extreme distance I would use a carp-type set-up with an in-line lead attached to a long length of anti-tangle boom, perhaps around 18in (45cm).

If you use really small baits such as an eel-head section or half a sandeel, you really can punch a bait a long way. With modern braid, a big-spooled reel and a frozen bait, 100 yards should be possible. I know this because I had to check one cast on the Great Ouse Relief Channel while zandering because I was going to hit the far bank (the Relief Channel is 100 yards wide). If you dry the bait off or shield it with a square of polythene you can also PVA it to the boom tube and this makes a very compact casting rig. It is, however, fiddly, which I refuse to bother with!

These days, if distance is required, there is a lot to be said for the use of a bait boat. These pieces of kit are expensive: my Microcat cost me about £600, but add an echo sounder to this, and you'll top £1,000. Needless to say, mine hasn't got an echo sounder, which doesn't worry me much. To be the ultimate, all-equipped pike angler probably means the pike hasn't got a chance of not getting caught. After all, it is supposed to be a sport. In the USA

they have underwater cameras to find the fish. I despair...

Regardless of this, as long as you don't have to carry it a mile, a bait boat can be invaluable – though I must admit that mine has yet to catch me a pike over 10lb. It has proved very helpful for carp, but since this is a pike book I should explain how I predict my bait boat will help me. Most obviously on some of the pits I fish there are areas I cannot reach by casting. Using the bait boat I can drop baits off by as much as 200 yards, which enables me to cover a lot of water. I use a reel with a big spool loaded with about 25 to 300 yards of either 65lb Whiplash or Daiwa Sensor Braid in 30lb breaking strain. I use plenty of lead to anchor the float-ledgered bait in place, and nice, heavy, drop-off bobbins. Used in conjunction with my favourite Delkim TXi Alarms I get instant registration if something picks the bait up. Unfortunately this is not a regular event at the moment.

Pike location is firstly a matter of finding the general area in a water where the pike are most likely to be, and there are certain golden rules that apply over and over again. Pike are designed as ambush pursuit predators: that is, they overhaul the unlucky prey by a lightning fast sprint from a standing start. The element of surprise is

A bait boat allows parts of waters to be reached that are out of casting range.

best gained with the benefit of some underwater structure that a pike can use as cover. A pike will not stay associated with the same piece of cover all day, every day, but will frequently move around during the day and the night. It is probably the period when the pike are moving that they are most likely to find your bait. In big still waters the most useful features are sharp drop-offs associated with shallower, often weedy areas. Humps caused by piles of rocks are standard 'must try' features. Pike

Location is important when deadbaiting. This Irish river pike of 20lb 2oz came from under an overhanging tree.

will frequent these areas in the winter, autumn and summer, only forsaking them for the shallows at spawning time. Not all waters have large amounts of underwater structure or drop-offs, in which case weed and reedbeds can then serve a purpose in providing ambush points.

Sometimes pike can be surprisingly close to the bank, but usually only where the margins are deep; they can also be close in near islands or underwater rock piles. Catching them in this situation is difficult if you are boat fishing, and generally

I'd tackle such areas with wobbled deadbaits or lures; in this way you can get right into where the pike are lurking. In rocky areas a ledgered deadbait would be asking for trouble; a free-swimming livebait might work, but generally the sort of water I am talking about will not allow you that option.

Rivers are always interesting in that pike are certainly not scattered around at random, and the more managed a river, the more difficult it is to pinpoint where they are going to be. A natural river in Ireland, on the other hand, is much easier to come to terms with. Deeper areas can be worth a look, but frequently the pike will be concentrated in the first shallower water adjacent to the deep water.

Bank-side cover can also be important. On one river I fished a couple of years ago the pike were holed up in a stretch that had a great many overhanging trees. Fairly obvious in a way, but for someone brought up on waters where overhanging trees were non-existent, difficult to relate to! The trick in these situations is to cast your baits as close as possible to the overhanging trees.

Fen drains are artificial rivers that are generally straight and featureless, but I cannot think of any drains that do not respond well to deadbaits. My approach is always to try and thoroughly search out the swim that I have chosen; it may be one where there are textbook features, which might include where other side drains come in, or big reedbeds where the rest of the drain is barren. Overhead power lines are also features, simply because dredgers tend to work these areas in a different manner, leading to a unique bottom structure near them.

To be successful you have to pick the right spots. This is a popular spot, but it can still produce.

129

A friend bends into a Fen pike that took a deadbait.

On all drains these days we are banned from fishing near power lines because of the risk of electrocution when long rods such as poles are being used. With our 12ft (3½m) pike rods we do not come anywhere near to touching power lines, but there is still a risk of arcing in damp weather; and casting over lines with wet braid is again not recommended. These areas can still be fished, but only with the help of something like a Microcat bait boat. Using one of these you can drop your bait off from a safe area without any risk to yourself.

Generally when fishing on the Fen drains that I favour, livebaiting is not allowed. Some clubs have banned livebaits, which isn't at all helpful, but then most of the club committees have no pike anglers

on them, so we get it in the neck as usual. So, equipped with my three or four rods and with a selection of deadbaits, I aim to start in an area I fancy and then leapfrog along the bank. I'll usually move a rod every hour, assuming that each rod has taken half an hour to cast out. So, for example, rod one goes out at 7am and is moved at 8am; rod two goes out at 7.30am, and is moved at 8.30. In this way you are constantly moving along, hopefully catching pike as you go.

In many situations you really do not need to leave a deadbait in a swim for more than an hour to an hour and a half; if a pike is hungry it will soon sniff out a bait, and then decide to take it. And if it is not hungry you are probably not going to catch it

Broadland rivers such as the Bure are excellent deadbait waters. This mid-double took a smelt.

in the short term anyway. It is rare that a 'sit and wait all day in one swim' policy works on a Fen drain, or indeed on many of the waters we fish. I nearly always float ledger on Fen drains. You only need two to four SSG shot to hold a bait in place, unless the drain starts to flow, in which case I usually fish substantially overdepth, and if necessary add more SSGs.

While the mobile form of static deadbaiting (no, that is not a contradiction!) on rivers and drains gives you plenty of exercise, on the broads you have to let the boat take the strain. Though there is plenty of bank fishing on the Broadland rivers, the mobility of a boat is all-important. I would never go to the Broads without being sure of being able to catch some livebaits while I am there. While deadbaits catch plenty of fish, you have got to be able to fish livebaits as well.

Some of the Broadland rivers such as the Yare, the Waveney and the Lower Thurne flow quite hard, and because of this the normal lightweight tactics employed on most waters have to be changed.

131

On fast-flowing waters it may still be possible to float ledger, but you need an ounce of lead to hold position. It is not a good idea to ledger from a boat, simply because fish that swim towards you may not be immediately obvious; far better to use a bigger float and more lead. In this way as you watch your float it will be clear when a pike picks up your bait.

A lot of pike anglers favour 'popping-up baits', which simply involves making a bait float off the bottom: in theory it will be more visible this way, and it certainly does no harm where weed cover on the bottom is extensive. Most people pop baits up using things like the fox-bait poppers. The little foam balls are wired to the treble, and in this way there is no risk of a pike swallowing the bait popper, which it might if attached directly to the bait. I tend to use pollan which, because their swim bladder is intact, makes them float as far off the bottom as you like. You can also suspend any deadbait using a float paternoster, and my biggest doing this is 34lb. To my mind a suspended deadbait is a far easier option than messing about popping baits up, but then what do I know?!

There's not a huge amount you can do to enhance the attractiveness of a deadbait from the scent point-of-view other than add a flavour or an oil. I am all for playing around in this way, though I frequently forget to take either the oil or flavour, or the syringe to inject the baits with! Perhaps I will get really well organized one day.

Most fish oils are not water soluble unless you use an emulsifying agent such as sodium laurel sulphate, but since this is the main part of many detergents, it is questionable whether or not you really want to add this to your bait. (Would you like Persil with your chips?) I think we have to assume that some small proportion of a fish oil is water soluble, and is what a pike will home into. Water-soluble flavours such as smelt will carry nicely in water. Grayling flavour is not very soluble in water, but the smell attaches itself quite readily to a deadbait, so a pike is going to know that it is picking up something different if you inject or even soak it in grayling flavour.

A simple way to increase a scent trail is to use a feeder packed with minced fish or make up rubby dubby balls using a stone inside, and freeze them. By throwing them into your swim you then have an instant scent trail. I remember a chap giving a talk at one of the NASG conferences years ago. He was using a muslin bag of blood and guts to attract the pike into his swim. In the end a pike actually tried to make off with the bag itself!

PREBAITING

Over the years I have done a lot of prebaiting for pike. The results have been highly variable, but despite this, the method is invaluable when it works. I've had the best success on gravel pits where the pike are a bit hungry. Cormorants can frequently deplete a water of food fish, and prebaiting works really well in these circumstances. This whole situation is a shame, in that sometimes you can have a pike that once weighed 30lb struggling to make a living and weighing in at about 25lb. By prebaiting we are to some extent helping pike like this to survive. On the other hand we are making these fish dependent on angler's baits. Nothing is easier to catch than a pike that has to take prebait to survive, but in these days of intense competition for good pike fishing it may well be the only way forwards. A serious prebaiting campaign benefits the pike, and can help them make considerable weight gains. On one water I fished, one particular pike started in September at 21lb and ended the season at 28lb 7oz. Some people would disagree

This sandpit twenty came from a heavily prebaited swim.

with this, but to my mind every angler who concentrates on his own water is one less out there on all the other pike waters.

To prebait a gravel or sandpit I normally try to find an area not fished by other pike anglers. This is not always easy, but really to make the method work you have to get away from other anglers, otherwise they will probably benefit from your efforts. How much you put in depends on how many pike there are in the water, and the activity of cormorants or eels. My initial

approach would be to throw in far more bait than the pike could manage on a weekly basis, and then fish after a couple of weeks. If I caught nothing I would gradually reduce the amount of prebait until I started to catch pike. I would judge 33lb (15kg) of prebait as a lot of bait, and 11lb (5kg) as being the bare minimum should pike appear to be in the area.

If the pike are very hungry then you will catch virtually everything in your particular gravel pit. This will also lead to repeat

A tiny bit of prebaiting two days earlier produced this Fenland 29lb 7oz.

captures, and it will be down to the angler to decide when to pull off the water. My view is that if you start fishing a water early in the season, say in October and they are hungry, you are going to catch those pike all through the winter over and over. The best thing you could do would be to not fish for them until the following February, and then they might be at their maximum weight. In order for the pike to improve in weight you obviously need to keep the pre-bait going in.

Sometimes the pike have the last laugh. I fish a large sandpit that has very limited access, and I can only fish three swims along one bank. I have tried the bait boat, but so far exploring a variety of areas has produced nothing. On and off from October I fished these swims, usually for a morning only, and I caught very little except the same low double – this in spite of regular prebaiting. Then around Christmas time I suddenly had a few fish, including an eighteen- and a nineteen-pounder. A week later I caught both of them again at just over 20lb and 19lb. Then the swim 'died', and nothing much else appeared.

Getting hold of large amounts of prebait is easier if you live near to a large fishing port; otherwise you can buy prebait from a business such as my own. All the packs of deadbait we sell generate a fair amount of waste, which includes mackerel heads, damaged fish, and fish that are too small. Prices work out at around £4 a stone plus carriage. You'll need a separate freezer of course for your prebait, so there is an initial start-up cost to a baiting campaign.

Waters where the pike are not as hungry will still respond to prebaiting, but you will find that once you have caught the pike from the prebaited swim you won't usually catch them again from that swim, at least not usually in the same season or year. My experience is that at some point the pike in the pits I have fished suddenly realize that there is free food available, and turn up and eat it voraciously. Usually I catch a few fish, sometimes with the occasional repeat, and then the pike will be gone.

Fen drains sometimes respond to pre-baiting, but unfortunately I have never had the chance to fish without competition, which has meant that several of my pre-baiting attempts have increased the weights of fish caught by other people. Sometimes where there is a lot of competition on a drain a mini prebaiting campaign can help you catch a big fish.

Last season I was finding things particularly hard going, and was hoping that as the end of the season came round the pike would move further upstream. I was down for three days and decided to throw a few damaged mackerel into one particular spot where I knew a fish in the 28 to 30lb class had regularly popped up. I fished elsewhere for a while, and then came back to the baited spot. It wasn't long before my float-ledgered smelt trundled off, and when I wound down it was obvious in the clear water that I had a good one. It went 29lb 7oz, and had last been caught at 28lb. It had weighed 30lb the year before and my extra food had obviously helped it back to near its top weight. I should have thrown in four more mackerel!

Unfortunately, heavier baiting of the same area did not give me any further rewards. Someone I know did catch the big fish – a thirty-seven pounder from just downstream from where I had baited. Whether it was my prebait that attracted it I'll never know, but competition and pre-baiting are poor bedfellows and I'd be inclined not to bother if there's a lot of it about. Sometimes prebaiting can be used as a defensive tactic if someone you do not like is fishing the spots you have found. What you do is fish the drain on the Friday and bait up with about 25 kilos of prebait. That effectively kills a stretch for at least a week. The trouble is judging when to go back and fish yourself. So far the tactic hasn't worked for me at all, but sometimes desperate times require desperate tactics.

There is also a little scope for light baiting while you actually fish. Throwing a few small baits or chopped larger offerings can induce a pike to look around for other food in your swim. I've always queried the theory behind this, however, because if the pike was already in your swim and feeding, it was bound to take a hookbait anyway.

DEADBAITS ON THE MOVE

Deadbaits do not have to be employed in a purely static manner. On a clear bottom it is possible to work a bait back towards you during a session; I know some anglers swear by twitching baits back towards them. A much more mobile technique is the wobbled deadbait. This is best performed with fresh baits, as they withstand regular casting better than frozen ones. As in all my fishing, I like to do things in a simple manner. I mount my deadbaits head up the trace with one hook of the top treble through both lips, and the other in the flank in such a manner that the bait has a slight bend in it. In this manner the bait slowly revolves through the water. Baits can be fished subsurface if you do not put any weight on the line, or deeper with the addition of SSG shot on the trace. Interestingly in the 1960s people were wobbling very large baits using multiplier reels and beach casters. That sounds like very hard work to me!

Wobbled deadbaiting can be a highly visible and exciting way to fish, especially if you are fishing over the top of weed. When a pike takes I generally wait a few seconds before winding down. Just as with any other type of bait fishing it is hook size that

is important. You should never be afraid to step up a hook size. The best way to miss takes when fishing for pike is to use too small a set of hooks. There is another thing to confuse us simple pike anglers, and that is the annoying way different hook companies have different ideas as to what constitutes, say, a size 6 hook. Half the 6s I see these days are really size 8s.

Baits for wobbling are, as I've said earlier, best used fresh, the most useful being roach and trout. However, any species of freshwater fish can be used, at a pinch. Perch are very tough and ideal for wobbling, and even last well from frozen. Smelt can be wobbled quite effectively despite the fact that they will previously have been frozen. The best fish to pick are the males because the big females tend to be full of eggs and are prone to exploding! I have even seen some chap in Ireland wobbling a great big eel tail section, which from a distance I thought was a Bulldawg!

Trolling deadbaits is a different game from wobbling baits. Generally we do not want the bait to spin in the water: steady, slow, rolling motion is all that is required. This we achieve by mounting the bait head up the trace, with one hook in the two lips and one in the flanks. This time we do not put a bend in the bait. I generally make my own anti-kink leads for trolling with deads from lead sheet. I simply snip out a circle and then fold it over the line above the trace. Before I do this I slide a length of silicon tube, the same length as the lead, up the line, and then fold the lead on to this. In this way the line is afforded a degree of protection from the lead, which might wear the line. The lead should be about an ounce (28g) in weight, and this will allow the bait to work at about 10 to 12ft (3 to 3½m) when trolling on tickover with the petrol outboard. There is seldom much need to go deeper than this because in clear water if a pike is going to have a bait it

Simple trolling rig using 1oz bullet, two size 2 or 4 trebles, and in this case a herring as bait.

will come up for it. There may be circumstances where you have to go deeper, but this is usually easily done by simply adding more weight and paying out more line.

If I have to put a lot of lead on to the line I prefer to attach it via a weak link away from the bait. To do this I have a 24in (60cm) up-trace and attach the weak link to the swivel connecting to the reel line. The weak link can be about 3ft (90cm) long, and is usually made from 15lb mono if using 50lb braid. You can put as much lead on this as you like, and though my only experience of using this set-up was on Lough Corrib while fishing for big brown trout, it seems to work quite well, with 4 to 6oz (113 to 170g) of lead holding the bait down at 40ft (12m) quite easily.

Usually petrol-motor trolling is carried out at around 1.5mph (2km/h). If you need to go more slowly then you have to float troll using either an electric motor or oars. These are my preferred choices, but there is one way you can troll really slowly on a petrol motor, and that is to fit what is known as a cavitation plate. This is a thrust deflector that can be tilted down behind the prop, and which diverts most of the thrust downwards enabling you to move very slowly. Tilt the plate up, and you can proceed as normal again. I've seen this system in operation, and it appears to work well.

My own experiences have mainly been with electric motors and oars. The aim using these systems of propulsion is to drag the deadbait under a float at about 1mph (1.6km/h). I use a large polystyrene float with an ounce (28g) of lead to keep the bait down. Sometimes I will increase the amount of lead to 2oz (57g), especially on windy days when it is difficult to keep the speed down. If you want to troll deeper but more slowly, I simply take off the float and hang the bait over the back of the boat. I try and get the line either vertical or at no more than 45 degrees, because in this way I know that the bait is working close to the bottom. The float-trolling and slow-trolling technique can also be used to fish livebaits.

With either live- or deadbaits, as soon as a pike takes, it can take line because the Baitrunner is set slack. I give the pike about ten seconds when using 6 to 7in (15 to 18cm) baits, and twenty seconds when using big baits over 10in (25cm). Then I simply wind down as fast as I can and bend into the fish. When using larger baits I'll often use the electric motor to accelerate away from the pike as I bend into it. Once

again it is important to use hooks of the right size. For anything of around 6 to 7in I prefer a couple of size 4 trebles, and if the bait is a tough one such as a trout, then size 2s can be used. I used to use extra strong Partridge or Owner trebles, but I've also had the chance to use some Gamakatsus, and these have proved reliable and not prone to straightening out.

IN SUMMARY

In conclusion the two methods of livebaiting and deadbaiting catch the bulk of the pike caught by UK pike anglers. If you want to keep things this way, you, the reader, need to be a member of the Pike Anglers Club and the Specialist Anglers Alliance. Both organizations have sites on the internet that will provide information on membership. Few of us want to be involved in angling politics, but as a pike angler it really is essential to protect our own interests.

5. Gordie's Adventures

by Gordon Burton

My lifelong passion for catching pike began when I was a very young boy, and right from the beginning every trip had an aura of adventure to it. In those far-off days it seemed that every waterway held log-like giants that ate everything in sight, and stories abounded of rod-and-tackle-busting encounters with huge fish. Back in those days at the beginning of the 1960s there was still a great deal of folklore and legend surrounding pike and pike fishing. My interest in fishing the huge waters of the British Isles was first stirred up when I began reading of the exploits of an angler who would become something of a fishing legend: that angler was Fred Wagstaffe.

Through the latter half of the 1960s and into the early 1970s, Fred was exploring some of Britain's biggest waters and coming up with some exceptional results. He wrote of his adventures in most angling publications of the time: *Angling Times* regularly featured his trips in search of big predators in a weekly column entitled 'Footloose with Fred Wagstaffe', and each week I eagerly awaited the next story. Throughout this period many truly enthralling articles unfolded, such as 'Pike from the Reeds of Cloonacleigha', 'Awe-Inspiring Pike' and 'Lovely Derg': adventures all of them, among the many I read, and ones I still have today. Fred described a pike as a 'power-packed bundle of fighting energy with bulging eyes and a toothy grin'! Prior to that time very little had been written about fishing these vast expanses of water and how best to tackle them, but Fred did it like never before – magic features and comments that were my inspiration both to fish and also to write about the big waters, and which would change my angling outlook forever.

Through reading Fred's accounts I became a versatile, tactical pike angler, always ready to tackle any water, however big, and alone if I had to! I exchanged many letters with Fred, but sadly, he is now gone. I feel it was a great pity that we never fished together. Today, all these years later, I still say that Fred was right up there at the top as the best pike-angling writer who ever lived – and I don't say that lightly, either. And there is another part to the story of my desire to fish these awe-inspiring places.

Way back in 1968 Dick Walker, along with that masterful pike-angling historian Fred Buller, travelled north to Scotland to visit an elderly gentleman who lived in Ross Priory, a stately house close to the shores of Loch Lomond. This man had in his possession the head of the now legendary 'Endrick pike' that had been found lying dead in the reedy marshlands, close to where the River Endrick, the river that gave it its name, flows into the loch. Walker had estimated that this preserved head must have come from a pike weighing a possible *70lb*! To me this was a quite staggering concept, and I believed in every

Fred Wagstaffe, a fishing legend.

ounce of it; and then in 1971 came the first of Fred Buller's classic books, *Pike*, that told legendary stories of Scottish and Irish pike of huge proportions – the 'Kenmure' pike, the 'Meelick' pike and the above-mentioned 'Endrick' monster amongst the many.

That initial feature by Walker really set my enthusiasm on fire: stories of Lomond pike stirred up the adventure in me, and that fire is still blazing today. The first time I ever saw great waters such as Lomond and Loch Ken the feeling was awesome, and even today every single time I push my boat out on to a vast sheet of water, another adventure begins: that is just the way it is! Over the years it has been my good fortune to have caught big pike from nine countries, and I enjoyed countless exciting and wonderful sessions that had me whooping with delight. In this chapter I will relate five adventures of fishing for pike, on big waters of the home country and far-off travels to the fly-to lakes way up in the north Canadian tundra. These involved fishing waters spanning a few hundred acres to vast lakes hundreds of thousands of acres in size: all great adventures for me, and I hope you enjoy reading about them.

A TROUT-WATER BONANZA

The trout-stocked lakes and reservoirs of Great Britain hold great attraction for many pike anglers, simply because these waters produce very big fish that have grown and waxed fat on an endless diet of the 'spottie' species. Over the years many pike anglers have questioned me as to why I have rarely been seen fishing on the trout-water circuit, travelling to fish every water that periodically opens its doors to the pike fisher. Well, for a start I hate to fish surrounded by other boats with anglers casting so close to me that it is possible to see the eyes on their lures. Not only that, but I don't like to pay extortionate prices for pike fishing on trout-stocked waters. My views on fishing these waters may surprise a lot of readers, but it is something I have to say, namely that fishing for big pike on any water that has been heavily stocked with trout, and with limited fishing access, makes these fish easy to catch! When any new water opens for fishing, the pike have been subject to no angling pressure at all and big fish are waiting to chomp everything in sight – well, at least the lures I throw! Let me loose pre-opening time, or at the start of fishing on any trout water, and I'll take it to the cleaners! It's rather like a big game hunter going to the zoo for his trophy! No, give me instead the vast and wild waters of the north every time. There have been times when I have enjoyed some very exciting sessions on

trout waters, and now I will tell of such an adventure.

In a violent fit of head-shaking madness a huge slab of a pike surged forwards, straight at the awaiting landing net. It was almost a disaster, as only its head and the lure it had smashed on to were enmeshed in the net before it went berserk and began thrashing wildly in the water. Realizing that it could rip free of the lure and be lost, I had to act very swiftly indeed, so I reached over the side of the boat, wrapped my arms around the fish's thick body, and hauled it aboard. Seeing how big it was I immediately let loose a mountain-shaking whoop! This great crankbait-chomping pike weighed in at 30lb 9oz – but little did I realize that this was to be the first of a fantastic haul of heavyweight pike all caught on crankbaits, or 'plugs' as we called them at that time.

This whole saga came about when a friend of mine, Gary Beecham, asked me if I would join him for an early morning trout-fishing session on Esthwaite Water in the Lake District. I fish for trout using large spoons and crankbaits, and had never been on the water in the pre-summer period, so my confidence was high, and I really fancied my chances of boating one of the water's big brown or rainbow trout. Over the years I have accounted for numerous specimen trout, super fish into double-figure weights, by using large lures, spoons and crankbaits – and I even took a 14lb ferox trolling a jerkbait. Many anglers no doubt scorn the use of such lures in trout fishing, but I chase the giant fish of the big waters.

There was also an ulterior motive, and I must admit to being armed with large artificial lures on this particular morning. I knew of Esthwaite's specimen pike population, and felt that one of them could be a possibility as well. A small selection of tiny Mepp's and Roostertail spinners for

A trout-water giant: 30lb 9oz.

catching table-sized eating trout, and about a dozen of my top big pike-catching crankbaits, were prepared for the trip. So I was well prepared to catch any big predator that came along, be it trout or pike.

Friend Gary had his own boat moored on the water, an extra bonus that allowed

for an early morning start to fishing. We arrived at the jetty and loaded all our gear aboard the boat in the pre-dawn darkness, and over a cup of coffee mulled over our plans for the day. First stop would be a shallow plateau shelving out from a spot known as Strickland's Field, a noted big

142

fish spot from where I had previously taken a pike close to 30lb in the autumn a couple of years previously. It was just after daybreak when I pushed the boat off and rowed off up the lake to the chosen location. The boat was then anchored in deep water out from the large shallow area surrounding the peninsula. The plan was simple: we cast the lures across the entire area from the shallow rocky shore out to where the water shelved away deep.

A fairly strong breeze was blowing up the lake and putting a good chop on the crystal-clear water. This wind, combined with a mayfly hatch and only a slight cloud, made the conditions, in my opinion, perfect for lure fishing, and I was very confident that fish would move from the deep water and hunt over the area. This view was corroborated before a cast had even been made when a huge pike suddenly struck the surface only yards from the bank. My confidence rocketed, and I immediately clipped on a large rainbow-trout patterned Whopper Stopper Hellcat Magnum crankbait and cast towards the huge vortex. Within a few turns on the reel the 30lb pike that I began this story with slammed its jaws hard on to the lure, and lashed on the surface before surging away into the deep water surrounding the plateau. A tremendous battle ensued as the fish strained my tackle to the limit. It seems amazing today, but at that time I was casting lures attached to 15lb test mono, in sharp contrast to the 30lb, 40lb and 50lb breaking strains of the braided lines I now use. Luckily all ended well and the fish was boated – and all the fish that came later! A few quick photographs were taken, and away she went back into the deeps.

After landing such a tremendous fish I was eager for, and confident of more action, and getting to grips with more big fish. Within several minutes of releasing the big one I was quite surprised when another toothy specimen took the same trout-patterned lure. At only about 6lb it was truly a voracious little devil, because less than ten minutes after I dropped it back into the water, it chomped the same crankbait once again! Any thoughts of casting the small spinners in an effort to try and catch a few 'takeable'-sized trout were completely dismissed when another very big fish struck on the surface. So it was to be 'all systems go' casting the large lures. Big pike were certainly on the prowl!

I need to say a few words here about seeing big fish movements on the surface. Whenever I am afloat on any large expanse of water I am constantly on the look-out for this taking place. Big pike that may appear to viciously body-lash on the top, just boil on the surface or simply porpoise through the waves. Whatever, I believe these are signs of hunting fish, and ones that are hard on the feed! I think that in roughish water conditions the higher levels will get well oxygenated, and prey fish move higher in the water and the big predators will hunt up there, too. It doesn't make any difference where big pike are seen moving, whether it is over areas of very deep water or in the shallows, they are mad when on the prowl – and the wilder the weather, the more aggressive the pike will be. Many are the times a big pike has hammered on to a lure after I have cast to its movements on the surface. So be warned: always be alert and keep your eyes open, and tame the 'high rollers'!

Anyway, back to the fishing adventure! Big hungry pike were on the prowl, and a few minutes after releasing that ravenous six-pounder, a big beast of a fish lashed across the water and struck on to a 5in (13cm) black-scale Predator Big Eyes crankbait my mate Gary was retrieving. It was another real hard-fighting fish, in superb condition and weighing in at 24lb, a very pleasing personal best for him. All this action was really firing me up, and I remarked to my companion that we could be on to a haul of big pike, and the likelihood of more 20lb fish. At that time I had taken two or more 20lb pike in a session on natural baits, but not on lures. Well, here was a chance to do it on lures, and being a great pioneer of UK lure fishing, to do it would be very special to me.

Hardly had the words left my lips when Gary's rod arched round as a big fish crunched on to a 7in (18cm) perch-scale Nilsmaster Invincible crankbait. 'Crikey, you have done it before me, you beat me to it!' I said, thinking he had hooked another big fish of over 20lb. It wasn't, however, and proved to be just a low double. But my dream was to come true very soon when in the clear water I saw a big fish engulf the same trout-patterned lure and, weighing in at 20lb 2oz, gave me my much sought-after brace of 'plug'-caught 20lb class fish.

A nice breeze blowing across the shallow flat and a mayfly hatch taking place was causing a regular showing of trout rising on the surface, which in turn was drawing the big hunting pike to patrol over the area. After releasing my last catch, I just had to sit down to have a cup of coffee and revel upon the fishing that was taking place, and to look forward to what else might be in store in the next hour or so, before it was time to leave for home, and work! I was soon back into rod-wrenching action, and in a short time boated fish of under 10lb, 10lb, 13lb and yet another heavyweight of 20lb. Due to the fact I was working my lures through shallow, clear water less than 8ft (2½m) deep, my choice was to use big slow-action, shallow-diving crankbaits. Trout? Well, a fair number did show throughout the session, and one big fish of around 7lb hurled itself clear of the water; but the 'spotties' were not in my thoughts as so many big pike were cruising the area and actively on the feed. We hadn't been fishing more than a couple of hours and we were bagging up, and four of the fish had been twenty-pounders.

Had Gary's work commitments not forced us to leave at 8am I am in no doubt whatsoever that had we stayed and fished throughout the day we could have possibly taken a real major haul of big fish. Analysing the session confirmed my long-held view even at that time, that big lures catch far more big fish than small lures. In this case I had taken eight of the ten fish on a 7in (18cm) Whopper Stopper Hellcat Magnum.

Thinking about what had taken place that morning I remarked to Gary, 'This is too good to miss!' On the return journey home I kept talking to Gary about the big pike and what the prospects could be if we went back again. So we decided to fish the water again the following morning to see if the big predators were on a prolonged feeding spell – and soon discovered that they were! It was still dark when I lowered the anchor in exactly the same spot as the previous morning. Weather conditions also remained the same as the day before. I shuddered with excitement as I clipped on the magic Hellcat crankbait, and made my first cast. Straightaway I struck into a tail-walking demon of a pike that went about 12lb.

And no sooner had we begun casting again, when Gary had a pulverizing strike on a perch-pattern Predator Big Eyes crankbait, and hooked into a very hard-fighting fish. At just short of 20lb it was a clear indication that the big fish here were mean, mad and still on the prowl. Working the lures with a slow retrieve was proving to be very effective indeed. A lure could easily be seen swaying its way back just beneath the surface, and the big pike were finding them irresistible. At times I didn't dare watch the lure as it was being slowly retrieved back, and so kept my attention on the rod tip in anticipation of an arm-wrenching strike!

Always a point worth mentioning is that a great many of these trout-fed pike are in a very overweight condition compared to those in most coarse fisheries. For example, they are nothing like as athletic and fast as the fish that inhabit the big Scottish or Irish waters. Working the lures slowly was undoubtedly the best way to tempt these big, ponderous pike, and if I did retrieve rapidly or in an erratic manner the fish could be seen to follow the lure right to the boat and either miss on the strike or simply turn away. It was truly exhilarating to watch a bow-wave heading towards the lure and see a big pike lash on to it in a frenzy of snapping jaws. After I returned that last big pike I decided to change lures and use a more varied selection. I did this really to get a few more of my lures chewed and battle scarred – lure fishers just love to show off boxes of their beat-up lures!

In no time I hooked into yet another very big one on a 7in perch-scale Original Rapala Minnow. Unfortunately, with an angry shake of its head it threw the lure free before battle even started. A quick change to a 14cm Rapala Magnum Special brought forth quick action in the shape of a big double topping 18lb, followed by another big one of 17lb that engulfed a chrome-pattern Predator Big Eyes. The action was coming quick and fast, and big pike were sighted exploding the surface in violent tail-lashing strikes, or a huge vortex would show close to the boat from fish that came near to the end of a retrieve. The hair on my neck was bristling, this fishing was so exciting. Our lucky streak was then somewhat compromised when Gary had a very big fish come off after a long battle.

Then I had the sickening misfortune to lose a massive fish. By this time I had switched back to the Hellcat lure, and the rod really whipped round as the big pike struck. The fish then lashed on the surface, causing the main line to wrap itself round its head, resulting in it cutting through – and it was even more upsetting because the Hellcat lure was still in its jaws! This fish looked to be in the mid-30lb range. And now we were thinking that this *must* be the end of such a fantastic run of big fish: surely there could not be more leviathans moving over this area? Well, there were!

Gary tamed another double, topping 12lb, on a Grandma lure. Then the Hellcat did it again, and a very big fish smashed on to the ever-effective lure and wrenched my rod down in the water as it sounded below the boat. Looking down at the pike as it swam below, in the clear water I saw a fish bigger than the thirty-pounder I had hooked the morning before! My 9ft lure-fishing rod was bent double as the fish tore off on deep, boring runs. It fought very strongly, but after about five minutes was in the landing net. Gary lifted it up on the scales: 'Thirty-one, thirty-two, thirty-three...' Then I spotted a big grin on his face: 'Sorry Gordie, it's only 28lb!' I verbally chinned him, then we took a few photographs.

By this time I'd had enough and stopped fishing, but nevertheless urged Gary on. 'Go for it Gary! You can have the spot to yourself, so get a beast!' Now what do you think of that for comradeship? Gary then systematically worked the whole area for quite some time before imploring me to have a few casts before we had to leave at 7:30am. And amazingly, in less than half-a-dozen casts another big pike crashed on the surface in a tail-lashing strike. The Hellcat Magnum had done it again, and my lucky streak continued with yet one more super conditioned specimen of 20lb coming into the boat. Five minutes later *another* big one broke free of the lure, and it was time to go; but I had boated a trio of

Gord plays a heavyweight pike!

twenties! It was like a dream, and I told Gary to give me a nudge to make sure I was not asleep! But no, I wasn't, and despite the lump on my arm where he hit me, I was still out on Esthwaite with a camera full of memories.

The pike were on a prolonged feeding rampage of jaw-crunching madness, and I had the uncontrollable desire to return once again in the morning. Gary couldn't do another early morning assault, but I had to get a cameraman this time. So a quick call to one of my piking friends, and the stage was set for another trip the next dawn; this time it was with John 'Fergie' Ferguson, who promised to video any fish I caught – and so he did! On this occasion I

planned to fish from the bank, while Fergie went afloat and anchored about thirty yards offshore.

Dawn was just breaking when I made my first cast. The chosen crankbait was a great favourite of mine, a $5\frac{1}{2}$in (14cm) Floating Rapala Magnum in silver mackerel pattern. This lure has given me lots of big pike over the years, and now it was about to notch up another one! A few casts and it was hit hard by a big fish, which at 22lb 4oz gave a great start to a short session – but it was soon to be seriously overshadowed! Due to poor light at this early hour I retained the fish in a tube. I then poured myself a coffee and sat on a boulder, gazing out across the mist-shrouded

A trout-water hawg! 31lb 9oz.

lake, wondering, what next? Conditions throughout all these sessions remained stable, so it was no surprise that pike were on the prowl; but these were the big stuff!

Once again I cast the deadly Hellcat out across the plateau, and it was *immediately* grabbed by a great beast of a fish: judging from boil on the surface it was obviously huge. As the pike cruised along just beneath the surface I was trying to gauge its size, when suddenly it exploded from the water, revealing a deep flank and broad back. Undoubtedly it was another 'thirty', and so it proved, at 31lb 10oz!

Thus in three short morning sessions not lasting more than a couple of hours I had accounted for fifteen pike, twelve in double figures, including five twenties and two thirties. At that time this trout water didn't have any lure size rule, and I exploited this fact to the limit.

A DELUGE OF RAIN AND A FLOOD OF BIG PIKE

It is April and early springtime as my young companion and I load my van and boat in preparation for the long drive up north to Scotland, to hunt the big pike of the wonderful, magical and mighty Loch Lomond. Young Colin Day had listened to me tell stories about pike fishing on this legendary water, and had been pestering me for quite some time to take him up there. Fishing the loch any earlier would have been tough going for a novice like him, simply because locating any numbers of the loch's big pike during the winter can be difficult, depending on the level of the loch. For that reason it was my decision to go in the springtime, and also because good sport would be virtually guaranteed. All of my past experiences told me that a blank session at this time was almost impossible. Confident? You bet I was!

We set off at mid-morning on the Friday, and as one would expect, the main topic of conversation concerned the huge catches of big pike I had taken with my friends throughout years of hunting and learning all about the feeding habits and movements of the loch's big fish. I had checked through my diaries of my previous years of fishing the loch at this time, and this told me that large numbers of specimen fish could be located in the shallow bays close to the in-flowing River Endrick. We arrived

in McFarlane's boatyard in the late afternoon, and just after we launched the boat it began to rain. We quickly got all our gear aboard and I motored out on to the loch; just south of the marina we anchored in the entrance of the Crom Mhin Bay, the scene of some of my amazing pike-catching sessions! It was my intention to remain afloat out on the loch for the whole of the two-day session.

Four rods were swiftly set up and cast into strategic positions, two baited with deadbaits and two with livebaits. Now anyone with experience of fishing in Scotland will be familiar with the fact this country is generous with rain: by this time it was really pounding down, and with just a couple of hours of daylight remaining I was preparing to sheet the boat over for the night. But at that moment a screaming run came to my rod baited with a whole herring. A quick strike, and the fish exploded from the water; a few minutes later, and a big double was hauled aboard my beloved boat the Creek Chub. At 16lb plus I let out a customary whoop as the fish was released. No sooner had I recast when runs came to two other baits, and soon both of us were playing a 'Lomond battler'. My fish of about 8lb was quickly brought alongside the boat and unhooked; Colin's was bigger, at just over 14lb, and he followed that one with another fish of about 10lb. What a start to the trip!

Now in the previous weeks I had been telling young Mr Day what can happen when Lomond comes alive. Only half an hour, and fish are coming fast. A quick tidy of the boat and two more runs occur: a good fish has smashed on to a big live roach on my rod and bolted! A similar run to Colin on a float-fished sardine turns out to be about 11lb while I net what looks to be low twenty – in fact not quite, it tips the scales at 19lb 4oz. A few quick photos, and with a lash of its tail away it goes – and away goes my float-fished herring: another strike! The fish rolls on the top and I turn to Colin and let out a glen-echoing whoop, telling him to get the net ready, because it's a big one! A real tussle ensues before the net is slipped under a beautifully marked pike. It was a little on the lean side, but it still weighed a very pleasing 23lb 4oz. What a start to a much talked about trip! Many times I have said that when Loch Lomond pike go on the prowl and the anglers in the boat are capable of handling a pack of marauding fish, a big haul is on the cards.

By now darkness had almost put its shroud over us; the rods were reeled in and baits put into the ice-box. I then took to the task of sheeting over the whole of the boat for the night, converting it into a floating bivvie! All the inboard water then had to be baled out before the waterproof mattress could be rolled out. Then out came the cooking stove, and I began the chore of cooking a lovely meal of Irish stew with crusty bread, and a pot of coffee. Sitting encamped in the boat I was revelling in thoughts of what the next day might bring. Seven fish had been boated in a short evening spell, so prospects did look good for the following morning.

While we talked during the night I had my lure box open, and selected a few of my great pike catchers in readiness for next morning's assault. The hooks were sharpened on a 7in (18cm) Rapala Magnum, a 7in Whopper Stopper Hellcat Magnum, and the ever-faithful wooden 8in (20cm) Creek Chub Pikie in gold scale, rainbow trout and perch scale patterns. These three crankbaits had all given me a great many big Lomond pike: the Rapala and the Pikie had both taken twenty-pounders from the loch. If the big pike were still on the prowl this coming session, then we were going to have a bonanza! At least, that is what I thought.

Scotland was really living up to its reputation for wet weather because there had not been the slightest let-up in this downpour since we arrived on the loch. Unfortunately when I sheeted the boat over, I hadn't covered the whole of the craft, and water was slowly rising up under the floorboards on which the mattress and sleeping bags were laid out. Soon, six inches of water was inboard, so I had to bale it out before everything got saturated. Colin snored the night away, but all I could do was cat-nap while the adrenalin flowed and the rain pounded on the plastic sheet covering the boat. At 5.30am breakfast was sizzling in the frying pan, and the teapot full of a piping hot brew. I took a peep out from under the sheet into the pre-dawn darkness, then got all the bedding and cooking gear rolled up and stored up front under the cuddy.

Dawn was just breaking when out went two rods baited with livebait, and two armed with float-ledgered deadbaits, either sardine or mackerel. When fishing the huge waters of the UK, I nearly always bait one rod with a great favourite of mine, a headless mackerel – a large mackerel with just its head cut off. This is a superb bait for big pike. Out went my mackerel into the middle of the bay, and Colin cast a sardine towards a weedbed close to an iron stake sticking up out of the water. I then began to cast the lures, but despite putting every ruse and twitch into a retrieve, not one single strike came to a lure.

Within a few minutes of the baits being cast out again, we both got a run on a deadbait. My fish went about 6lb, while a low double had come to Colin's sardine. Several small fish came to livebaits, then Colin got a take on a live roach, and judging from the way his baitrunner reel was screaming away it had to be a big fish – and so it proved, at exactly 20lb!

A super streamlined pike of 26lb 4oz.

So Colin's first trip to Loch Lomond, and he was seeing extremely good action, and had caught a twenty-pounder too. Still the rain persisted, and not drizzle but lashing it down. The water level was starting to rise, and the River Endrick was fast flooding; past experience told me that dirty brown water would soon be spreading across the shallow sandy flats out from the river, and would affect the whole southern basin of the loch. The big pike of these normally clear-water lochs will not tolerate dirty floodwater, and will turn off the feed. But luckily for us, the wind had been blowing from the south-east for the past few days and had pushed the dirty water away from our fishing area – and the pike were still mad on the prowl.

Whilst combing the area with a lure, another double of 14lb came to a headless mackerel. Whilst unhooking the fish I managed to retrieve the bait from its jaws, so I trimmed off the tatty, shredded flesh from the bait and recast the remaining piece, about 4in (10cm) long; a small-sized bait, but because there appeared to be a lot of pike moving and feeding hard, I felt it worth a try. Sure enough, it was picked up by something extremely powerful that porpoised on the surface on its initial run, and a tremendous battle followed before it was netted. Though long and lean, it was still a super fish, and a mountain-shaking whoop greeted its weight of 26lb 4oz on the scales.

More and more fish came to the boat, both small ones and low doubles. Oh, and the rain had still not let up for one minute! I had to continually bale water from the boat, otherwise it would have been full to the gunwales! Another big double of 18lb-plus came to my whole herring, followed closely by a twelve-pounder to Colin, which was followed by a handful of smaller fish. Pike were still in abundance, so I made the decision to stay the night and fish the early morning period before packing up for home. It was another long night of pounding rain: when would it stop? In past years of fishing Lomond I had endured some appalling weather, in fact whatever conditions it threw at us, but I'd never seen rain pour down as relentlessly as this deluge. I had a long, restless night as I lay there listening to the weather of Scotland do its worst. With dawn not far off, the customary fry-up of egg and bacon was cooked, and washed down with cups of hot coffee. Then on with the waterproof gear, and off with the cover of the boat to face the constant deluge of rain; but would the flood of big pike continue?

Colin Day and a pike of 22lb 4oz.

Another Lomond beauty: 21lb 8oz.

Hardly had the baits settled in the water when I struck into a tail-walking demon that tipped the scales at just over 17lb. A few minutes later and I was in action once again, battling with another sky-walker that smashed on to a live roach and left the water in a gill-flaring leap before I even struck the hooks home! It was another super fish, topping 20lb at 21lb 8oz. Yes indeed, the flood of big pike was still on the go! More small fish came, then Colin struck into a fast-running fish and I could see it was another of 20lb plus; so I eased off the pressure on the clutch of his reel and instructed him to take it steady. A few minutes later I netted a beautiful fish that went 22lb 4oz. Colin was 'on a roll', and he soon hooked another big, hard-fighting fish, again to a livebait – but sadly it broke off at the boat-side.

By this time the wind had changed right round to a south-westerly direction, the water in the Crom Mhin was clouding fast, and the pike would eventually 'turn off'; but anyway we had finally got to the end of our fishing time, and had to pack up and depart for home. Our total haul had consisted of over thirty pike, with fourteen of them in double figures, and five of over 20lb, for over 3cwt (152kg) of fish. I will forever be speculating just what we may have caught had the rain not been so heavy and flooded the loch. Many anglers are very critical of fishing in wet conditions, but all I can say is, if pike didn't feed in the rain on Scottish lochs, they would spend a lot of time not eating!

During the whole time that we were continually catching pike on natural bait tactics I had been casting lures whenever possible; yet amazingly, not one single pike followed or struck at a lure. The water was clear, and no more than 4ft (1.2m) deep in the whole area the baits were being fished. Over many years of pounding the waters across the mighty Lomond and other lochs, I have experienced some super sessions both casting and trolling lures, and have finished up with numerous big fish in a single session; but the lack of interest from big pike on this trip was truly extraordinary, and remains a mystery to me to this day. Having fished the loch so often in previous seasons I had experienced longer sessions that involved catching bigger pike, and much larger numbers of fish. This short sortie produced marvellous results continually, throughout appalling rain-swept conditions. No rainbows were seen, but we found a pike-fishing pot of gold!

A PREVIEW TO MORE ADVENTURES

The two above stories were about exciting sessions when big pike were really mad on the prowl and feeding hard, and I was lucky enough to exploit the situations and take big hauls of fish. The next two stories are not just about catching lots of big pike, but were intense fishing sessions in which I would learn all about the feeding habits and movements of the big fish on Windermere, England's biggest lake, and on Loch Lomond, Scotland's biggest loch. To many pike anglers such big waters are a daunting challenge, when really this isn't the case. Windermere was so easy because I was a piker of long-term experience of fishing huge waters. Lomond was different

simply because I was exploring the unknown, and at the beginning of fishing a vast and awesome water. Here I tell of these adventures.

A WINDY SURPRISE!

It was a cold and bleak late January morning the first time I pushed my boat the Creek Chub on to the waters of Windermere, England's largest lake. Looking back, I can't think why it took me so long to make this move, but it was no doubt due to the fact that Scotland and the great lochs were considered much more attractive, and the prospects of catching very big pike far better. For those reasons, I and many other pike fishers took the long journey up north, and for many years bypassed this Lake District water. But from time to time snippets of news concerning decent pike caught from the lake came to my ears, until finally I decided I should give the water a look over.

Not knowing a single thing about the lake, and because it is a big water, I first took a trip to check out launching sites. A motor boat was hired at Bowness, and accompanied by my young son Walker, I travelled all around the islands to the east shoreline; here I had been informed there was a shingle bank where it was possible to launch a boat.

It was a few months later before I finally set out to fish the lake. Besides the obvious procedure of studying a map of any new water before fishing it, I also had a plan of how best to tackle it for the first time. For many years now my initial tactic of finding out about a water, and of locating pike-holding hotspots in particular, is to troll, simply because trolling is a high speed method that allows me to cover large areas of water more quickly than any other tactical approach. Not only that, but trolling is a method that has been a great favourite of mine for many years now, and gives me the long-term results I want: even in the harsh conditions of winter, trolling will still pull up the beasts!

So here I was a decade ago, afloat on Windermere on a January morning for the very first time. Using large spoons and crankbaits on flat-line and lead-cored lines, I combed the deep water north of the islands in the middle reaches of the lake for the whole of a bitterly cold morning, but without a single strike at a lure. Scanning my map of the lake I took note of a large area of shallow water south of the ferry line that crosses the lake from Bowness on the eastern side of the lake. In the afternoon I headed into the southern section of the lake to troll over this wide area of mid-lake shallows. By this time a blizzard of snow was sweeping across the water, and the wind was like a knife cutting into my face: certainly fairly bleak conditions to troll in!

I was pulling two shallow-running crankbaits – a 6in (15cm) Grandma in Fire Tiger pattern on one rod, and a 6in Pikie pattern Nilsmaster Invincible on the other – when the first strike came, a small fish smashing on to the Grannie lure. I steered the boat across a deep-water area to the eastern side of the lake to check out some rugged-looking shoreline, and here came the second strike to the same lure. This was also a small pike of about 6lb – but I was soon to be in for a big surprise. Yet again I motored over deep water, cutting back across to the east side of the lake, and began trolling a stretch of water between a peninsula and an island. Wham! Here was a wrenching strike, with the rod bent double in the outrigger rest. I grabbed the rod and pulled into what was obviously a big pike – and so it proved. A fantastic, fat conditioned specimen and as good-looking a pike as I ever saw that hit the scales at 23lb.

A loud whoop echoed through the distant hills. Would this fish be a lucky fluke? Time would tell. I couldn't wait to tell my long-time piking friend Frank Pennington, a seasoned big-water pikeman, of this quick success on a forgotten lake. A couple of days later Frank and his friend Eric Draper went up to give Windermere a go, and that night, Frank rang me excitedly: 'Gord, wait for this! We got six pike on the troll, five over 20lb, and four of them over 25lb, with the best 28lb!'

What a catch! And all those big fish took crankbaits. This was almost too good to be true, and I was eager to get back there. So a couple of days later my old piking friend Gary Beecham and myself were on the water again, exploring far and wide in the northern half of the lake; and once again trolling lures was my chosen approach. After carefully studying the map I selected a long stretch of productive-looking water to work the lures over for several hours. We started by trolling over the 30ft (9m) contour, pulling an ever-faithful Creek Chub Pikie and an 8in (20cm) deep-diving Cisco Kid; but we never had a strike in the first couple of hours. So I then switched to a different depth level, using a tactic I had invented myself and called the 'step up' or 'step down' approach, according to whichever way I might be working lures through the depth levels. We switched to shallow-diving lures, a Pikie pattern 6in/15cm Nilsmaster Invincible on my rod, while my companion clipped on 7in (18cm) perch pat Rapala Minnow.

In a short space of time two big doubles of 16lb and 17lb smashed on to Gary's lure. He remarked to me, 'You'll get a big one, just you see.' Well, I steered the boat very close to the extremely rocky shoreline to begin turning round for another run back over the area, when suddenly there was a vicious jagging on my rod, which at first I thought was the lure bumping the

A winter pike on the troll: 24lb 8oz.

rocks; but then the rod lashed round as a big pike slammed its jaws on to it. *What* a fish it was, a super fat 24lb-plusser! That big fish told me conclusively to give this water some real attention, and to locate and exploit the pike-holding areas on the entire lake: and so another adventure began.

Instead of just trolling, as the first sessions had been, from here on it would be 'all systems go', because besides trolling in a session, I would also bring livebait and deadbaiting tactics into action. Soon after taking that last twenty-pounder I was back again, and this time I searched over the area where I took that fish; I found it to be a super pike-holding hotspot at that time of the year, and in the winter generally – and, as I later discovered, at any time! This location has great fish-holding features: a rocky reef reaches out from the shore, there is a large inward-sweeping turn, a sharp drop-off close to the shore into 20ft (6m) of water at one end of the bay, a gradual sloping off at the other side, and super weedlines in the summer.

The boat was positioned in the middle of the bay, and deadbaits were cast to various spots while I combed the area casting jerkbaits. A crunching take in 30ft (9m) of water produced a fat seventeen-pounder to a fluorescent perch-pattern Dolphin, then at mid-day a take came to a whole mackerel. What a battle followed the strike, and only a good ten minutes later could my friend Frank Pennington get the landing net under a tremendously hard-fighting pike. Had this fish been as fat as the two 'heavyweights' I had caught in the previous few weeks it would have weighed in the mid-30lb range; but never mind, it still went 29lb 8oz.

In the coming months we caught plenty of big pike, including twenty-pounders, continually trolling large areas of the lake and also fishing static tactics over new features I had picked up on my sonar unit. The more spots that were tried, the more big pike were caught. It was also evident from my sonar work that Windermere is home to huge numbers of perch, charr, eels, trout and more recently roach, all super forage fish for the pike to prey on.

The one consistent feature in the capture of these fish was that the majority of them were caught in a similar depth of water, that is between 25 and 30ft (7½ and 9m). Throughout the winter periods that I fished, the fishing was slow, and there were many one- or two-fish days; but usually there was a big twenty-pounder as a result of the regular stints put in on the water. I don't mind trolling for long sessions if a horse of a pike is the outcome. As the springtime progressed, more and more big fish were caught in shallower water, but this was usually close to noted spawning bays. In the early summer weedbeds were located in certain areas, and if the 'green-stuff' was found close to rocky features and steep sloping drop-offs, this spelt a 'big pike' spot in capital letters. Either casting or trolling close to deep weedlines was magic fishing, and lots of big fish hammered my crankbaits in style.

In the mid- to late 1990s very few pikers were seen on the water, and so the fish were subject to little pressure; as a result, myself and a couple of close friends had a bonanza, and twenty-pounders were often caught. It was during this period that my friends and I first took livebaits to the lake. What a treat was in store when putting this method into practice! I lost count of the times I got on to the lake at dawn with a bucketful of livos, and two or three hours later had none left, but had landed a pile of pike. These catches always included a good number of fish into big double figures. I well remember a lad who had never caught a twenty-pounder asking me to help him catch one. I said that if he paid the fuel bill for three trips to the lake with me, and if he didn't catch one, I would give him all his money back! Well, it was early July, and all the weedlines were lush and green, and pike were really on the go!

Dawn had not even broken when I anchored the *Creek Chub* in 18ft (5½m) of water out from a deep weedline close to a rocky drop-off. No sooner had the baits hit the water than they were snapped up by marauding pike. Several small fish into low doubles came in rapid succession. Then 'high rollers' began to show as big fish were seen striking on the surface. We began casting lures over the area, and young Cal quickly struck gold: a big pike smashed on to his lure, and after a good fight and a few panic attacks from its captor, I hand landed what was quite obviously his 20lb dream. At 21lb, he had done it first time out with me!

A fifteen- and an eighteen-pounder quickly followed, and then I hit into a big one that pulverized a perch-pattern Super Shad Rap. A few minutes later I had it in the boat, a super 25lb 12oz giant of a pike. To give the fish a rest it was suspended in the water in the landing net over the side of the boat. I then picked up my other lure rod armed with a Nilsmaster Invincible and made another cast – and it was hammered straightaway by *another* big one! It could be seen clearly deep down in the water fighting hard, but soon I had it in the boat, a super fish of 25lb 4oz. What a brace! The two fantastic specimens were photographed in my arms. It was just 8.30am, and we then left the water: it was time for work! All this water and hardly a fisherman in sight!

Non-stop exploration was taking place, and I was learning more and more about the lake and giving all the hotspots a name: thus were christened 'Frankie's Hump', 'Draper's Drop-off', 'Gordie's Island', 'Sunken Bay', 'Alcatraz' and 'Bucket Island'. I remember one chap saying to me, 'I bet you can draw a map of what the lake is like under water!' 'Not far off!' was my reply. My view of using the sonar gear is to study it carefully and take everything in; this is vital if you are to learn all about the topography of a venue. Windermere's pike feeding patterns were always noted, and so it was often easy to work out when big pike could be caught.

It is also no surprise to locate small packs of big pike in some locations, and for this reason throughout the spring to autumn period a 'run and gun' approach is a great way to fish: that means hitting as many spots as possible in a day, mostly casting lures but sometimes in conjunction with bait rods. This tactic gave me some tremendous days. Once day I was afloat with two chaps, and as we drifted towards a weedline I warned them to be prepared, as I knew this was a great spot! On my first two casts, using a Bulldawg, I took two 20lb class fish, and this was followed by several doubles and another twenty. This is a big, daunting water and difficult to tackle, but not so when you take the logical route via habitat study. The pike of these big lakes have a wide choice of habitat.

More and more pike anglers descended on to Windermere as the word of its fishing spread, but many struggled to catch fish. Some people think Windermere can be a moody venue, but this is not so. One must be widely versatile in order to be consistently successful. How many anglers are fishing in depths of 30 to 45ft (9 to 14m) and often much deeper? In my view this is deep-water habitat that few anglers will exploit – yet I have lost count of the big fish I have caught in such depth bands when trolling lures.

There are two main features that greatly affect success with these pike, and these are floodwater conditions and algal blooms.

Such elements undoubtedly put a damper on the fishing, and the pike will not feed. Catching numbers of big pike during heavy rain is never a problem, but when it causes the level of the lake to flood a couple of feet, the result is they go off the feed. Why? I suspect all the run-off from the surrounding towns affects the water, and it always pays off to wait for the level to drop back to normal, usually three or four days. Algal blooms are a real hindrance, and pike will not tolerate them at all on big, clear lakes. I fished the lake often enough to know these facts.

By the year 2000 I knew the whole lake really well, and I started the year catching a 20lb pike on the first trip of this new millennium – and on the second trip, and the third trip, too! This amazing fishing continued as I landed one or two, and once three 20lb-plus pike on eleven consecutive day trips to the lake. In one period I had caught twenty pike, and ten of them were in the 20lb class. This was fantastic fishing, and Windermere, through all of my fishing explorations, gradually became a place where I expected to catch a 20lb pike every time I went. There was one amazing two-day spell when I caught seven twenties on lures and deadbaits, though none topped 24lb. I even managed to hit a little purple patch while fishing for a film camera when making a video.

Livebaiting was banned, but I am still catching lots of big fish using other tactics. Only a few days before finishing this story, a friend and I boated fourteen pike in one morning, all on deep-trolled crankbaits. The fishing is exceptionally good, and I hope to continue exploiting its water for a long time to come. Who knows? Perhaps you are regularly by-passing a big lake, or any water that appears to be devoid of pike anglers, or little is revealed about the place – so give it a try! You may go on an adventure like my 'windy surprise'!

THE MIGHTY LOCH LOMOND

It was after reading about the now legendary 'Endrick' that the idea of fishing this magical Scottish loch first stirred my imagination. Loch Lomond was home to monster pike, and the great Dick Walker had written about them in such an awe-inspiring way, and this was soon to be the place that was my burning desire to fish. It was during the summer of 1972 that I travelled up to the loch for the very first time with a couple of non-angling friends just to take a look at the water that in the future would captivate me more than any other place. I can vividly remember standing on the jetty at Balmaha and gazing at the splendid scenery and out across this immense sheet of water: I was utterly dumbfounded. I had written to Walker numerous times in previous years for advice on fishing the loch, but now I realized I didn't have the all-round knowledge at the time to tackle such a mighty place. The lowland lochs I had fished before seemed like mere puddles in comparison to what I was now looking at. To gain experience I fished other lochs such as Ken, Auchenreoch, Urr, and even the huge Loch Awe. Many good pike came to my rods, including a twenty-pounder from Loch Ken.

At last in June 1974 I felt confident enough to return to Lomond. A boat was hired from Balmaha, and during a five-day session I took eleven fish, including three doubles to 16lb 14oz, the best succumbing to an 8in black-jointed Creek Chub Pikie. The fishing was fantastic, and how the fish fought! Had the biggest one come off I would have sworn I'd lost a monster. Whooping with delight wasn't a part of my fishing at that time, but I was over the moon. A couple of trips in the late autumn

Gord crossing the mighty Lomond.

only brought small fish caught by my late brother Barry. In the spring of 1975, Barry and I returned again and the result was a very exciting session with fifteen fish to 18lb 3oz being taken on dead roach and perch, and Creek Chub Pikie and ABU Hi-Lo crankbaits. This type of piking was really firing my enthusiasm.

More trips later in the year again resulted in just small fish being caught, but in the next trip in the spring of 1976 Barry and I enjoyed another grand session, taking thirteen pike including three good

ones to 16lb from the Crom Mhin Bay. In the summer of that year I received a letter from a certain John Watson – yes, the famous 'Wotto' – who suggested we team up together for future fishing trips; he especially fancied the prospect of fishing Lomond. But our partnership got off to a shaky start when after a couple of nights' eel fishing I was struck down by the deadly Weil's Disease virus and almost died. Fortunately I was strong and tough, and intensive care in hospital saved my life.

Just after I left hospital, Wotto and I accounted for one of the biggest hauls of zander ever taken at that time from the River Delph in Norfolk; but the sessions took me to the verge of exhaustion because I was still so weak after my time in hospital. My thoughts again focused on Lomond, and John suggested we go up to fish the loch every weekend. This involved a round trip of 500 miles. The thought of this was magic, and I couldn't sleep the night before setting off for thinking about those tremendous pike we would soon be catching. Although we got off to a slow start, we

had the Lomond bug, and in the following weeks we took a stack of big pike – and lucky for me, all the real 'heavyweights' came to my rods.

Whenever I am afloat on any water it is always my policy to cast lures as much as possible. Well, late one afternoon Wotto and I were in Crom Mhin Bay when a big pike lashed on the surface between his rods. Quick as a flash I grabbed a lure rod and cast a Creek Chub into the fading vortex – and the fish slammed its jaws on to it. I gave my whoop of joy: it was a magnificently proportioned fish of 20lb! But John

Gord back in the 1970s with a Lomond twenty-pounder.

was rather annoyed that I had cast over the area he was fishing, and so there was a prolonged silence!

To demonstrate my confidence in using just lures, the next trip was spent casting and trolling lures, and no bait fishing. This trip proved successful for me as I took the most fish: eleven in total, although I did put a deadbait out during one rest period, and a double tail-walking fish of 20lb 11oz took it. The fishing was so good we often ran out of baits. (Neville Fickling might just recall an instant when I ran out of baits, and while going past his boat I had a cast with a Gudebrod Sniper lure, and hooked and landed a hard-fighting fish that weighed just under 20lb!)

Travelling up to the loch was a very tiring affair, leaving Southport at 7pm on a Friday evening and arriving in the early hours of the morning. Jimmy Pairman the boatman was very friendly, so much so that after one bitterly cold session he gave me half a pint of whisky. After drinking that, I ended up in a collapsed state in the back of the van. He also let us dry our wet clothing on the heaters in the boatyard workshop.

At the start of this campaign to extensively fish Lomond, the only two other specialist pikers I had encountered were the late Slim Baxter, and Chris Bowman. They would become part of the group of anglers who later came to grips with fishing the

Loch Lomond in winter.

loch the whole year through, and they accounted for many big pike. At this time, very little angling pressure was put on Lomond; however, things were to change drastically in the coming years. Due to my successes I began reporting catches to the press, and later wrote articles myself; features such as 'The Lomond Challenge', 'The Lomond Thriller', 'The Glory of Lomond' and 'Raiders from the Deep!' were among the many I wrote. Debates raged regarding the record potential of the loch, and this publicity led to large numbers of anglers travelling to fish the loch – but most anglers only fished the loch in springtime, when the pike were in the shallow bays to spawn. Lomond was continually in the news.

At the end of the 1970s my fishing began in earnest, because I teamed up with two forward-thinking anglers, namely Rob Forshaw and Kev Fairclough. We began the first winter's campaign in fine style, with Kev taking an incredibly hard-fighting pike of 28lb; it took a big carp livebait while we were fishing in deep water beyond the mooring buoys out from Balmaha harbour. Apart from watching the prolonged battle this big pike put up, I can vividly remember this winter's day as being the coldest session afloat I had ever endured – my feet felt like blocks of ice! The area around Balmaha was frozen over at dawn, and we had to break our way through the ice to reach the open water. Periodically through the day snow blizzards swept the loch – it truly was a bitterly cold day: in fact it was an endurance test, sitting out there alone in an open boat.

At this time Rob and I were planning to do something never done before, and have an all-year assault on the pike of Loch Lomond. Fishing up there through the whole winter was something of an unknown adventure! Dick Walker said weather conditions at times would make

fishing impossible, but in fact that only occurred a couple of times, though we arrived in Balmaha to find deep snow and the loch completely frozen over! So eager were we to go we didn't even check weather forecasts, we went anyway! Truly we fished through some of the most atrocious conditions imaginable; but more of that later.

Once the decision was made to explore the whole loch in the hope of finding new hotspots, we would spend time studying the Admiralty chart of the loch and pinpoint new places to try each trip. It seems amazing today, when using my top notch Bottomline Tournament Champion sonar unit, that back then I found many new locations without the use of any type of echo sounder, and often using a sliding float set-up to plumb the depth! Incredible! We were going up there week after week, so often that it had become an obsession!

On most of the trips, nights were spent afloat on the loch in order to be ready for action at the break of dawn. When I motored across Lomond at the start of a new session the feeling was electrifying as my eyes scanned the water, thinking '...down below swims the ultimate pike'. In complete contrast to fishing Windermere twenty odd years later, at this period in time I didn't have much experience in searching out pike hotspots on such vast expanses of water – but now I was to embark on such a venture. At the beginning of each trip I would fish a known place in the hope of getting a few fish, and then I would try an area never fished before.

It was also essential that we took the best livebaits and deadbaits possible up there for each trip. Top quality baits meant success, too, and we used what I term a 'saturation approach': two or (rarely) three rods each, fishing natural baits and casting lures. It was left to Rob and me to troll far and wide across the loch hoping to pick up fish in remote areas, and to find another hotspot. Slowly but surely more and more hotspots were pinpointed, and twenty-pounders were caught from all around the vast southern basin of the loch. We fished in depths never before fished, taking pike from below 40ft (12m) down on baits, while I caught fish by trolling lures more than 50ft (15m) down. I discovered that using silver livebaits such as roach and dace would well outscore the darker-scaled species such as perch and carp; and in the summer period I also found that livebaits and lures would far outfish deadbaits. It was very exciting fishing indeed, so much so that when a run developed, my legs would shake in anticipation that a monster pike had taken the bait. Working as a team, Rob and I revelled in our fishing and took some incredible catches of Lomond pike. For instance, one assault produced forty doubles and five twenty-pounders for over 650lb of pike.

The prospects of catching a giant pike of over 40lb was something I dreamed of and talked about a great deal. In April 1980 Slim Baxter really set my enthusiasm on fire by taking a magnificent 34lb 12oz giant in Portnellan, close to where Tommy Morgan caught a 47lb 11oz giant, and where Fred Buller also lost a monster. A few dedicated friends joined in the Lomond assault; my late brother Barry was always up there, and my friend Frank Pennington in particular became a very adventurous piker, and put a great deal of thought into his fishing. Right through to the mid-eighties, Rob and I continually hammered out amazing hauls of pike: hundreds of double-figure fish, and dozens upon dozens of twenty-pounders and fish topping 30lb were hauled aboard the *Creek Chub*. One short session produced 441lb of pike! There is no doubt that we took the biggest catches of pike I have ever heard of

being taken from the loch! By selecting good-looking features such as rock points off islands, deep bowls or humps in the loch bed, and remote weedbeds, and using the right tactical approach to catch fish, I gradually gained the confidence to tackle anywhere on the Lomond – or anywhere at all, for that matter. One very important point when fishing a huge water such as Lomond is that pike may not be active in one location, but in a bay several miles away they could be rampaging and chomping everything in sight – and then a big haul of fish is a distinct possibility! This was something I found out on a regular basis when exploring Lomond.

Right from the early days of fishing the loch I experienced the ever-changing weather conditions: fishing there so often, I faced the full brunt of Lomond's elements, and at times it was hellish! One winter's night Rob, Frank and I were camped on the shore close to the Crom Mhin Bay. Shortly after we settled in our sleeping bags it began to pour down with torrential rain; it went on for hours, but because we were fast asleep we didn't realize the level of the loch was rising fast. When we had arrived on the loch in the afternoon there was thick snow on the surrounding mountains, but the amount of rain that fell overnight washed it all down into the loch, causing it to rise two feet! We had to get out of our sleeping bags very quickly and suspend all our gear off the floor, because soon water was swirling around our ankles – and it was only 2am! A raging gale lashed the loch for most of the day, but during a lull in the storm we got afloat for the last hour before dark, and I hit into a super fish of 24lb 8oz.

Despite the conditions in the night the adrenalin was flowing, and I was eager to get back the following week. There were times when we arrived at Balmaha to find the loch frozen over, but smashed our way

A big winter twenty-pounder.

through ice in order to fish! No moon boots in those days, and sometimes it was freezing so hard out on that loch that icicles formed on the rods! Those who have seen my slide shows will know I fished through all conditions, and even raging gales! It was a long time ago when I first started out, and I wanted to learn all about the feeding habits of Lomond pike at a time when only a few of us fished the loch all year. Many times I arrived at Balmaha and asked Jimmy how the loch was fishing,

and he would say '...you are the only chaps I have seen in weeks'. Lomond had a magical attraction during those early years, and there was a wonderful camaraderie between those of us who were fishing the loch at that time. This really was the pinnacle of my pike fishing, and surely unsurpassable! I can well remember talking to Slim Baxter shortly before he sadly passed away, and he said '...the Lomond era was the greatest period in pike-fishing history': and he was right; and I was there!

TO THE CANADIAN TUNDRA, AND THE WORLD'S BEST PIKING

'Take it, go on take it!' I urged while watching a big pike come bow-waving after the lure I was retrieving along the surface. Suddenly the fish exploded from the water in a jaw-snapping frenzy and engulfed the lure. Magic! This kind of action is, in my view, the very pinnacle of lure fishing for pike. To be able to stalk lots of big fish in clear water conditions is indeed one of the greatest delights in lure fishing for pike. Events like this are treasured by keen lure enthusiasts – though it is a very lucky angler indeed here in the UK who can watch, let alone catch large numbers of big pike from clear water. Now imagine seeing a hundred – yes, I did say *one hundred* pike! – in a day come chasing after lures retrieved to the boat while it drifts across shallow clear-water bays, and not only lots of small ones, but plenty of fabulous speckle-marked big fish topping 20lb.

On many occasions I have been asked '...where in the world is the best place you have ever been pike fishing?' Well, for seeing and catching big pike in numbers nothing remotely rivals what I experienced when I visited Wollaston Lake and the

Cooking shore lunch on Wollaston Lake island.

neighbouring fly-to-water Ahenekew Lake situated in the northern area of Canada's province of Saskatchewan. I had previously seen film footage of amazing catches of big pike from remote lakes in Canada in various videos imported from the USA, and the thought of ever fishing such places was just in my dreams – but dreams do come true!

Over the years I have enjoyed some fantastic piking throughout Britain and parts of Europe, but I never saw so many big fish in such a short space of time as I saw on the Canadian lakes. I was initially based at a place called Rowan's Ravine Lodge situated on Last Mountain Lake in the lowland area of the province, and had been enjoying catching some cracking walleye and some fantastic speckled pike to around 20lb. This trip was part of a three-week trip across Canada, and besides the other species I also caught a great number of big carp, some largemouth bass and muskie.

A two-and-a-half day-trip sortie north to Wollaston Lake came as a complete surprise, and I was revelling in the thought of flying out to fish a vast lake in the far north. Absolutely magic! Taking me on this dream trek was Ted Hornung, one of Saskatchewan's tourist chiefs, and Martin Founds of Angler's World Holidays. The first stage was a four-hour drive north to the town of Saskatoon where we boarded a plane and flew north to Prince Albert and then to La Ronge. It was truly amazing looking down over so many other famous Canadian pike waters, such as lakes Athabasca and Reindeer that could be seen on the next stage of the flight north to Points North airstrip. No matter which direction I looked down from the plane, the landscape was the same as far as the eyes could see: flat, and with fir trees by the billion!

It was at this remote place that we boarded a coach that transports fishermen to Wollaston Lake Lodges. Situated just a hundred miles (160km) south of the Arctic tree line, Wollaston is a truly vast water: 110 miles (180km) north/ south, 45 miles (72km) wide, and with about 2,700 miles (4,345km) of shoreline, plus 370 islands. In fact it is the twenty-third largest lake on earth, and is 270 miles (435km) from the nearest town. Another surprise is the fact that the lake is frozen over for a large portion of the year. Although in Canada and the USA it is quite the accepted thing to do to eat small pike and walleye – I have done so myself during my trips to these countries – big pike are different, however, and Wollaston was the first of Canada's largest lakes to receive a 'catch and release' designation from the government. Furthermore, fishing with barbless hooks on lures is compulsory for anglers using this campsite. Besides teeming with pike there are also vast numbers of predators, walleye, arctic grayling and lake trout, too.

We finally arrived at the camp just before midday, and were directed to a well constructed log cabin and prepared for our first session on the lake. All the tackle was set up, and we were introduced to our guide for the two-and-a-half day's fishing, Rob 'Crash' Mullins, a seasoned veteran who worked with thirty other guides in this camp. It was at this stage that I was to get my first shock: I was to be ferried by floatplane to a distant lake over the tree tops. All the gear was loaded and I climbed aboard. Sitting there in such a small craft I was somewhat worried about flying out over the treetops when suddenly 'Hap', the pilot, turned around and asked 'Who is the English guy?'. When I said 'It's me', he told me to come and get into the co-pilot's seat and help with the controls, as he needed help to fly us out! What a way to start off my trip! It was an awesome sight, the water racing by as the plane sped up the lake and into the air.

Loaded and ready to fly out to big pike.

A short flight over the trees and we touched down on the calm waters of Ahenekew Lake and cruised to the shingled shore of an island where a number of aluminium boats and engines were permanently moored up. The tackle was hastily loaded on to a boat, and we set off to fish in the mouth of a tiny inflowing river where we were soon catching small pike and walleyes. 'Crash' told me to keep several for the group's shore lunch later in the day. Then we set off to hunt pike in earnest. We cast out spoons as the boat drifted slowly along the shoreline, and the action soon started, with fish after fish crashing on to the lures. It was hair-raising indeed to see so many pike moving close around the

boat, before they followed and struck at a lure. A great number of small and medium-sized fish, and plenty of big doubles in the 16lb to 18lb class were seen, and some heavyweights in the 20lb range. What an exciting start it was, with so many fish smashing on to my lures that it cost you fish if you wasted time weighing them. I was quite happy with that anyway, and would know a twenty-pounder if I got one! Just like the big muskies I have caught in Canada, the pike are also judged by their length and girth measurements, and there are so many fish that unless they are big ones, weight is a bit irrelevant. Due to the sheer numbers of pike in these waters, this is something I can fully understand. I

A beauty caught on a spoon.

would love to see how Neville Fickling would cope in these situations where there are so many fish being caught, when he weighs all he catches!

At the end of the first session both Ted and I had taken a huge number of fish on a whole variety of lures, with Martin recording much of the fishing with his movie camera. Ted had taken most of his on Daredevils and Len Thompson spoons, while I

caught pike on crankbaits such as the Reef Hawg, Rapala's Super Shad Rap and Husky Jerk, Hi-Fin Scamper and Storm's Thunderstick. Many of my fish also took spoons such as the Professor, Rasenen, Red-eyed Wriggler, and two of my home-made Jim Vincents (copied from one that Derrick Amies, the one-time holder of the British record pike, had lent to me) painted with the Two of Diamonds pattern.

Hunting pike in shallow bays.

Amongst the many pike I caught were some crackers around 40in (1m), with one of 41in (1m 2cm) that was a definite 20lb class fish; that particular specimen was caught from fast-flowing water in the mouth of the Umpherville river that links Wollaston with Ahenekew (named after an Indian chief) lake. I have the whole capture of the pike on film, from the cast and the strike, then playing and hand-landing the fish. The bait that was proving to be so effective was spoons with a bright fluorescent orange and Chartreuse yellow pattern, although I recall that one very big fish in the high 20lb range followed my large silver and gold Red-Eyed Wriggler spoon, but unfortunately declined to smash on to it. This short morning stint was electric: never had I seen so many fish moving in clear-water conditions – and did I just absolutely love it!

At mid-day we stopped fishing and two boats motored to a nearby island where the guide cut up a pile of brushwood and set up an open fire on which to cook for the team of five. The feast consisted of beans, sweetcorn, chips and the tastiest walleye and pike fillets you could wish to eat! A real treat in a great adventure – those North American guides certainly know how to camp cook. After lunch I was back in the cockpit of the float plane flying back to the lodges.

After a good shower and freshen up in the cabin, we all departed for the main lodge dining room for a superb evening meal. We then retired to the lounge bar to chat with all the other fishermen and discuss the day's sport, how many fish were caught and the big ones that got away! The walls of the lounge are adorned with fantastic replicas of huge pike and lake trout. You can also help keep your adrenalin flowing by watching the films of fishing on the lake. Many of America's famous fishermen regularly visit Wollaston, and I met Babe Winkelman who has his own 'Gone Fishing' show on television in the States. The day had passed very quickly, but what a day it had been! Ted and I ribbed each other about who was going to catch the biggest pike of the trip. Would the new assault be any better? I was to be astonished.

The next morning after breakfast we boarded the plane for another fly-out, but this time it was to a distant location on Wallaston known as 'Sandy Bar'. In the first drift we covered the shallow bays where there were big pike in abundance, but most of them approached in an inquisitive manner, rather than in an aggressive lure-chomping mood. Lots of big pike trailed behind the lures right to the side of the boat, but showed no sign of striking. And don't waste your time trying to 'figure of eight' the lures: it is a very rare event for a pike to strike at a lure being worked in this way. Using Polaroid glasses was very important, because not being able to see the fish in the clear water would have been a real disadvantage.

Why these big fish were in this mood didn't take long to work out. These shallow bays hold little in the way of prey fish, and I saw nothing other than big sucker fish. However, a number of the pike I caught still had white fish in their throats, and regurgitated tiny fry and larger samples when they were being unhooked. All of these big pike had been feeding in the deep-water areas in the early hours of the morning, and had then retreated up into the back of the shallow bays to rest up and digest the food in the warmer water. On most of the waters I fish back here in the UK I would not expect to find so many big pike in such shallow locations other than at spawning time. Wherever I went out on this great lake there were loads of big pike; in fact some of the places where we tracked numbers of big pike really did surprise me, because they were far, far back in flooded muskeg swamp. This is obviously down to changing weather conditions and prey fish, which in turn govern the feeding habits and movements of the big pike.

Although fish were caught steadily throughout the morning session, in the afternoon sport became electrifying: the pike had digested their early morning meal, and went on the rampage! They were striking lures in a way I had never seen before, and it was tremendously exciting to watch big pike surging after spoons as they fluttered and danced through the water. I also used a trick that I'd never used before, namely to cast a broad-shaped spoon and keep it moving across the surface in a zig-zag style on its belly. 'Show boating' is what I termed this new idea. Pike came after top-water lures (Woodchopper, Mr Twister and Jitterbug) retrieved at high speeds, repeatedly striking at the lures if they missed...and all caught on film! At the beginning of the session I was counting the numbers of pike as they were being caught, and it didn't take long to reach fifty, and

A fantastic speckled 43in fish from the Canadian north.

lots of them big ones; Ted would often be hauling out a cracker of a fish at the same time as I was.

It was amazing to drift into the tiniest of bays and find it loaded with big pike in violent, aggressive mood. Sometimes I saw as many as eight fish up to about 20lb in a single tiny area! It was in these spots that came the most surprising experience of all: I would cast a spoon close to the overhanging brush and begin a rapid retrieve. A pike would come after it in a tail-lashing wake and smash on to it. What a shock I got when I hooked a fish that immediately came off, only for it to turn on the lure and strike again! Sometimes a fish would hit a lure hard a few times before getting a proper hold. I would be talking to the pike, willing them to strike: 'Come on, come on, it's dinnertime and show time, take it!' Sometimes there would be two or three pike following a lure at the same time. 'They're following in shoals!...' I exclaimed at one time: just like I had seen in those American videos, and now I've got film footage doing it myself.

It was in one of these tiny bays that I learned a 'new' trick from 'Crash' the guide, and boated two big pike. The first one came rocketing after a spoon just when it was being lifted from the water, but instead of dashing off after this abortive strike, the fish just slunk away slowly. At this point 'Crash' told me to fit a 10in (25cm) rubber worm and skirt rig on to my trace, and then jig it across the pike's path. Well, what a whoop I uttered when its mouth opened and engulfed it on the first cast, and soon a big double was being hauled aboard the boat. I have since used this trick many times on my home waters.

Ten minutes later two more big fish swam past the boat, and it was easy to see they were well in excess of 20lb, with the biggest of the two around 4ft (1.2m) long. They had moved about ten yards (10m) when I cast the worm between the two fish: the smaller of the two turned on the worm, opened its great jaws and sucked it in. I whooped for joy: what a pike, a fabulous speckled specimen, 43in long and with a 19in girth.

This turned out to be the best fish of the two fly-out trips, and it beat Ted's best by an inch. We had good fun ribbing each other over how friendship can be divided by such a short dimension! Big pike were showing so often that I panicked if a lure got tangled up, for fear of missing out on a fish. Even at the end of this incredible trip, pike were chomping lures almost as fast as I could cast them out; it was just amazing!

It is not uncommon for a fisherman to catch ten or more twenty-pounders in a day, and every season fish over 30lb are caught. Oh, and the season in not much more than two months is due to ice over! At times I felt a quieter approach would have been better in order to prevent spooking big fish. I felt at times that 'Crash' was a bit reckless, but because there are so many fish you can get away with it. The number of big waters in Saskatchewan is truly an absolutely remarkable 98,000, and many of these lakes are just loaded with pike. Just think about that next time you are sat on your local water; but I realize I have fished a pike fisher's paradise!

Appendix

British Pike Over 40lb Since 1950

Weight	Captor	Venue	Date
46lb 13oz*	R. Lewis	Llandegfedd Reservoir	October 1992
46lb 8oz	A. Stewart	Oaks Fishery, N. Ireland	March 2005
45lb 15oz	D. Willingham	Barnes Fishery	February 1999
45lb 6oz*	G. Edwards	Llandegfedd Reservoir	March 1990
44lb 14oz*	M. Linton	Ardleigh Reservoir	January 1987
44lb 8oz	C. Garrett	Llandegfedd Reservoir	October 1988
44lb 2oz	M. Lawrence	Barnes Fishery	February 2000
44lb	S. Gilham	Llandegfedd Reservoir	October 1988
43lb 2oz	P. Wright	Castle Howard Lake	1988
43lb 2oz	B. Ingrams	Llandegfedd Reservoir	October 1988
42lb 12oz	P. Harvey	Blithfield Reservoir	July 1988
42lb 8oz	A. MacPherson	Martnaham Loch	1964
42lb 8oz	P. Malcolm	Loch Fad	April 2005
42lb 5oz	P. Climo	Llandegfedd Reservoir	October 1988
42lb 2oz*	D. Amies	River Thurne	August 1985
41lb 12oz	J. Costello	Undisclosed	January 1994
41lb 12oz	C. Bailey	Bluebell Lakes	February 1995
41lb 12oz	M. Godfrey	Bewl Water	January 2000
41lb 8oz	D. Amies	Thurne System	February 1983
41lb 8oz	R. Dixon	Bewl Water	December ????
41lb 8oz	E. Edwards	Blithfield Reservoir	October 2001
41lb 7oz	M. Cooke	Blithfield Reservoir	November ????
41lb 6oz*	N. Fickling	River Thurne	February 1985
41lb 4oz	J. Mills	River Thurne	February 1986
41lb 4oz	N. Williams	Surrey Stillwater	January 2005
41lb	M. Espin	Birchmere	January 1994
41lb	C. Bailey	Bluebell Lakes	February 1995
40lb 12oz	N. Williams	Bluebell Lakes	February 1996
40lb 8oz	T. Simpson	Bough Beech Reservoir	December 1991
40lb 8oz	G. Moreland	Oaks Fishery, N. Ireland	2005
40lb 6oz	M. Hopwood	Kent Lake	November 1979
40lb 4oz	K. Vogel	Loch Ken	1972
40lb 4oz	E. Raison	Rookery Lake	February 1994
40lb 2oz	S. Marshall	Bough Beech Reservoir	December 1991
40lb*	P. Hancock	Horsey Mere	February 1967
40lb	M. Cooke	Llandegfedd Reservoir	October 1996

* These fish have held the British Record as determined by the British Record Fish Committee

Index